John Pritchard is Bishop of Oxford and was formerly Bishop of Jarrow. He was Archdeacon of Canterbury and, before that, Warden of Cranmer Hall, Durham. He has served in parishes in Birmingham and Taunton, and has been Diocesan Youth Officer for Bath and Wells diocese. Other books by the author include *The Intercessions Handbook*, *The Second Intercessions Handbook*, *Beginning Again*, *How to Pray*, *Living Easter through the Year*, *How to Explain Your Faith* and *Going to Church: A user's guide*. He is married to Wendy and has two married daughters.

D1394204

THE LIFE AND
WORK OF A PRIEST

John Pritchard

First published in Great Britain in 2007

Society for Promoting Christian Knowledge
36 Causton Street
London SW1P 4ST

British Library Cataloguing-in-Publication Data
A catalogue record for this book is available from the British Library

ISBN 978–0–281–05748–1

5 7 9 10 8 6

Typeset by Graphicraft Ltd, Hong Kong
Printed in Great Britain by Ashford Colour Press

Produced on paper from sustainable forests

*Dedicated with affection and respect to the
priests of the dioceses of Durham and Oxford*

Contents

A word at the beginning   ix

1 What kind of love is this?   1

Part One
THE GLORY OF GOD

2 Presiding genius? Exciting the imagination   11

3 Spiritual explorer: Passionately directed
   towards God   22

4 Artful story-teller: Opening up a world of grace   32

5 Multilingual interpreter: Exploring the
   landscape of faith   40

6 Inquisitive learner: Digging into theology   49

Part Two
THE PAIN OF THE WORLD

7 Pain bearer: Keeping vigil with a damaged world   59

8 Wounded companion: Sharing the journey   67

9 Weather-beaten witness: Discerning the Kingdom   76

10 Iconic presence: Identifying with the community   84

11 Friendly irritant: Challenging the structures   91

Contents

Part Three
THE RENEWAL OF THE CHURCH

12 Creative leader: Scanning the horizon   101

13 Attractive witness: Pointing to Christ   111

14 Faith coach: Helping people to grow   120

15 Mature risk-taker: Thinking outside the box   129

16 Flower arranger: Managing the church's life   139

AND FINALLY

17 Life-fulfiller: Enjoying all God's gifts   149

Further resources   161

A word at the beginning

When I was a vicar in Taunton we had a very good church school a mile or so from the parish church. The children didn't therefore come to church as often as I came to them. In school I would wear a clerical collar but not a cassock, and the children were used to seeing me around the classrooms and in assembly. On one occasion, however, the younger children came to the parish church for a service and I was in a cassock. I stood at the door seeing them out and one little girl looked up at me in amazement. 'Mr Pritchard,' she said, 'are you pretending to be a vicar?'

That question has haunted me ever since.

I sincerely hope I haven't been pretending to be a priest all these years, but what actually should I have been doing? Priests come in such different varieties; they speak such different languages; they have such different priorities. There's no one-size-fits-all model of being a priest. Writing about the life and work of a priest is therefore a dangerous venture. No-one will agree with me for a start. I'm bound to reveal my prejudices and blind spots. I might be rumbled at last.

Many books have been written about being a priest. Some are mainly theological and some more practical. Some have become classics, such as Michael Ramsey's *The Christian Priest Today*, and some have been well read for their sheer common sense, such as Robert Martineau's *The Office and Work of a Priest*. This book pays homage to the latter. *The Office and Work of a Priest* was first published in 1972 and was much valued as a wise account of the duties of a priest at that time. Many of those duties of course are timeless, but the context of the Church today (in particular the Church of England from which I write) is very different; and this book reflects both a different era and the different personality of the writer, but it owes its origin to the inspiration Robert Martineau gave to very many priests and would-be priests some years ago.

My aim has been to write about the principles and practices of a priest's life and work. It's the book of a jobbing bishop who's in contact with many parish priests every week and whose own ministry came to life as a priest in that parish in Taunton. The slant of the book is undeniably towards local parish ministry, although I hope there is considerable overlap with the life and work of sector priests, self-supporting ministers and ministers in secular employment, and certainly I mean to include many generic principles of ministry for those involved in 'emerging' forms of church. Fundamentally, I believe there is no higher calling, and nothing more valuable, than to be a priest in the service of God and God's people. The pay could be better but that's another matter!

Bishop Jack Nicholls was once told by his spiritual director that the only things he had to be concerned with as a priest were the glory of God, the pain of the world and the renewal (repentance) of the Church. With his permission I'm using that three-fold division as the shape of this book. You'll note that God and the world come before the Church. That seems to me to be an important signal. We serve an astonishing God for the sake of an amazing world; we're not simply church functionaries.

When I took on one new post my excellent secretary gave me a card on the front of which was a circus tent with a dog balancing precariously on a unicycle on a high wire. The dog had a hula hoop round his waist; in his mouth was a cat; on his head he was balancing a vase and at the same time he was juggling several balls. The caption read: 'High above the hushed crowd Rex tried to remain focused. Still, he couldn't shake off one nagging thought; he was an old dog and this was a new trick.'

That is how it seems to many priests these days. Ministry is changing fast and to some priests the Church of today is hardly recognizable as the Church into which they were ordained. For some that's a source of bewilderment and even disillusion; for others, including those coming fresh to the life and work of a priest, it's a source of stimulus and challenge, adapting to a 'mixed-economy Church' of both inherited models and fresh expressions. But there is one thing that I want to maintain with as much grace and encouragement as I can: the goal of ministry will always be the same – that men and women in every place may have life in all its fullness and abundance.

And that fullness and abundance is meant equally for the priests of God's Church.

After writing the first draft of this book I entrusted it for comment to a group of people in whom I had great trust, and they didn't disappoint me. I am indebted to Stephen Cherry, David Day, Peter Eaton, Ruth Etchells, Judy Hirst, Ian Jagger and Gordon Oliver for the wisdom that has saved me from much folly and has greatly improved the text. My wife Wendy is always a splendidly fierce and loving critic and my editor Alison Barr has, as ever, been a patient, helpful and experienced guide. My thanks go to all of them. I'm also delighted to have a number of Ron Wood's wonderful cartoons to lighten the text and remind us not to take ourselves too seriously.

One comment they made with varying degrees of robustness was that the picture of the priest that emerges from the book is a bit too busy and breathless. With such a crowd of witnesses I can only plead guilty but it isn't my intention. I have high ideals for priesthood, certainly, but the most important chapter for me is the one on being a spiritual explorer. Anything that emerges from our ministry that isn't rooted in prayer and love is likely to be dark and empty. Priests have to be signs of stability in a bewildered world. They have to be God's priests before they do priestly things. Forgive me if I seem to ask too much.

Having said that, I trust what follows is both a hopeful and a realistic survey of the life and work of a priest as the twenty-first century gathers pace. I shall be more than pleased if an older generation recognizes the contours of their God-given task, and if a new generation is encouraged to take up the challenge. I believe there is no more exciting and necessary vocation.

John Pritchard

1

What kind of love is this?

I wonder who inspired you most in your early Christian life? All of us have at least a modest hall of fame containing affectionate portraits of people who not only inspired us but also genuinely helped us to raise our game and try to be better persons. Among these portraits might be a priest. Again, I wonder what it was about that priest that affected you so much? There may well have been something special about them – a quality of life or a sense of their being 'fully alive'. I think of a priest I knew in my early teens who was full of fun and laughter and deeply engaged with the young people around me, but whose centre of gravity was obviously elsewhere, somewhere much more special that I only dimly recognized. (He was also the priest who first said I ought to think of being ordained, an idea from which at that time I recoiled in horror.)

These special people, whether ordained or not, have a distinctive quality that we find hard to pin down. They tend to be kind, though not in a sentimental way; they tend to be selfless, though not with martyr-like complications; they tend to be strong characters, but they use their strength creatively for others. They have a kind of fullness about them, an expansive humanity, an invisible source of energy. As we think about these people more carefully we might find eventually that we're using words like holiness, the chief outward characteristic of which is love.

Being a priest might be described as a kind of loving, a way of deploying the love of God for the well-being of others. But what kind of love is this? Some people reading this book may

The new curate was a little shy at first

be starting on the road towards ordination and be asking that very question. 'What kind of Love is calling me, and what kind of love would I be called to offer?' The process of discernment they have set out on is both complex and delightfully simple. It's complex because (in the Church of England) he or she has to see any combination of the vicar, the Diocesan Director of Ordinands, a Vocations Adviser, a local diocesan panel, a bishop's examining chaplain, and eventually the advisers at a national selection conference, now called a Bishops' Advisory Panel. On the other hand the process is delightfully simple because what the candidate is essentially doing is tuning in to God's call and staying on course towards God until he or she discovers just what it is that God wants.

So how does the Church answer the question about what kind of love this priestly ministry really is?

Selection criteria for ministry

The Church of England has nine criteria in its discernment and selection process. Other Churches would have a similar list. They come across as rather functional descriptions but they contain much accumulated wisdom.

Vocation. Candidates need to be able to speak realistically about their personal journey of faith and how they have come to feel they may be called to ordained ministry.

Ministry within the Church of England. Candidates need to show that they understand and appreciate not only their own tradition in the Church but also the traditions of others. (I rather like the idea of us all being called to a ministry of 'intelligent evangelical catholicism in the power of the Spirit', which neatly combines the traditions we often separate out as liberal, evangelical, catholic and charismatic. But we all quite properly have our own emphases.)

Spirituality. Candidates will need to show that they have, or are developing, the spiritual resources necessary to sustain them through the demanding experiences of public ministry. Are their spiritual disciplines robust and life-giving?

Personality and character. Candidates have to demonstrate maturity and self-awareness, the ability to handle change and also to welcome it in themselves. Honesty and integrity are vital.

Relationships. Candidates need to be able to recognize their strengths and vulnerabilities, and be able to handle complex relationships and expectations with maturity and integrity.

Leadership and collaboration. This is a new and necessary criterion, requiring of candidates the ability both to offer leadership and to foster the gifts of others and put them to good use.

Faith. At first this sounds obvious, but it means an understanding of the Christian faith and a desire both to deepen it in oneself and to communicate it to others. Personal commitment to Christ is essential.

Mission and evangelism. Another new and necessary criterion, this one looks for a wide understanding of what mission means in a changing culture, and an ability to communicate the Good News meaningfully and attractively.

Quality of mind. The Church is looking for people with the necessary intellectual capacity and curiosity of mind, together with a commitment to being a life-long learner.

This is a very useful list of criteria and makes me wonder how I ever came to be recommended for ordination! However, it's still a fairly functional answer to the question of what kind of love this business of being a priest really is. I once went on retreat and was met by a little bundle of holy energy who showed me to my room. I thought I'd better start in prayer but as I knelt before a crucifix in the room I began to feel worse and worse. I realized that I needed to do a lot of soul-searching. I knew that over the years I had accumulated quite a lot of experience of priestly ministry. I knew about pastoral ministry and mission; I'd served on synods and working parties; I knew a bit about church law and how to stay out of trouble. I'd been involved in parish work, youth work, theological education and was now an archdeacon, and I realized with growing horror that I could do all of these things, if I chose, almost entirely without reference to God, except as a code-word or cipher. I had the experience and the skills to get by without God. Of course I didn't want to, but it was a stark warning that priesthood is much more than a set of competencies. No accumulation of skills impresses God. God is interested in the heart of the priest, more than in how impressive his or her CV appears to be.

Why might God want priests?

So let's approach the issue from the other end. Instead of looking at what a priest needs to be able to do, let's look at why God might want priests at all. One way to approach this question is to start with the nature and character of God.

God is by very nature a missionary God. Mission isn't an activity that God sets alongside other activities; it's the very nature of God to reach out to the world in creativity and love. Theologians have a phrase for this: the *missio Dei*. The life of God constantly overflows exuberantly into the world from the godly play at the heart of the Trinity. So far so good: God is forever in mission mode because that's God's nature.

Jesus embodied God's mission in the world, and therefore his life, death and new life have given Christian faith its characteristic shape and goal. Jesus didn't just show us what God is like. As well as being God's self-portrait ('like Father, like Son') he also enacted the central drama of God's mission by draining evil of its power on the cross and launching God's new creation in the resurrection. God's mission is completely Christ-centred and that's what has always made it so exciting to me. I've always found the figure of Christ fascinating, compelling and irresistible. It's this wonderful figure that we commend.

It follows that all mission and ministry belong to Christ, who now works through his Body the Church to continue to set before the world the love of God and the new life that has become possible through that terrifying cross and astonishing resurrection. The Church is the baptized community, constituted by the blessing of Jesus Christ. The baptized people of God are then sent out to love and to serve, to offer the blessing of Jesus afresh in every arena of human activity. At the same time we in the Church keep our celebratory heart focused on the eucharist, in the light of which all life is blessed and challenged. We know we'll never fully understand the eucharist; we just know it's absolutely essential (by whatever name we know it – Mass, Holy Communion, Lord's Supper). The Church continues joyfully to present Christ to the world, and can be recognized by the four defining characteristics of the creed where it's called to be 'one, holy, catholic and apostolic'.

All ministry is Christ's ministry, therefore, but it's exercised through the baptismal vocation of all God's people, in the power of the Spirit. All this is highly compressed theology but I hope you follow where we're going.

Only now in this theological white-knuckle ride do we arrive at authorized ministries such as those of bishop, priest and deacon. They exist only to serve and support the ministry of all God's people. Essentially they are *representational* ministries. They are signs of the ministry that is alive and well in the Christian community. So, for example, it would make no sense to have ordained deacons if active service doesn't characterize the whole worshipping community. Nor would it make sense to have priests if the whole community wasn't a priestly people. Authorized ministers represent the people of God and have no existence independent of the rest of the Body of Christ. The priest is no more the Church than the Prime Minister is Great Britain – a mistake often echoed in the repeated phrase that so-and-so is 'going into the Church'! Nevertheless, the priest does represent and focus the ministry of the Church at key times and in key ways, as this book will explore. We still need to remember, however, that finally the priest is someone who has been dazzled by the beauty of God and longs to reveal that beauty in the world.

All this theological description is a bit like looking at the score of a Beethoven symphony and trying to imagine what it sounds like in a concert hall with an orchestra in full flood. It's far better to experience the living embodiment of the bare description – whether the subject is a symphony or a priest. What we can say, however, is this: ministerial priesthood is God's gift of love both *to* the Church and *from* the Church: *to* the Church to enable it to live up to its calling, and *from* the Church to make the love of Christ known to the wider community.

Let's leave concepts behind and think of an image instead. It's as if God is the supreme Artist who invites us into his studio. He gives us a huge choice of paints and some rough sketches of what he's after (like the Sermon on the Mount or the glimpses we get in the parables). He promises to be constantly available as tutor, adviser and friend, and then he says, 'Let's paint!' Because this is a long-term project he also appoints a few people to act as convenors of the painting workshop, not because they're any better at painting than anyone else but simply because he calls them. And so we get on with the great commission, not 'painting by numbers' but rather painting 'after the style of Christ' – the Artist's equally gifted Son. In every church in the world, in every locality and in each life, the painting goes on . . .

The life and work of a priest

This book employs a range of images to give new life to conventional categories of priesthood. The first set of images clusters around the way the life and work of a priest seeks to honour the glory of God. The second set of images focuses on the priest's relationship to the needs of the community and the wider world, with all its ambivalence and pain. The third set of images looks to the priest's role in the life and renewal of the Church.

However, one thing needs to be emphasized from the start. Through all the categories and images of the book we should be able to hear the steady heartbeat of the call to holiness. No part of the life and work of a priest can prosper without the constant, daily renewal of the sacred centre of the priest's life. Prayer, scripture, sacrament and fellowship are the essential resources the priest returns to day after day, week after week. That's where true joys are to be found.

What kind of love is this? It's a love that prays.

Part One

THE GLORY OF GOD

———◆◆◆———

God of glory and unquenchable Spirit,
may your Son direct us afresh to the fire of your presence
where nothing may amaze us more than your love,
      nothing may inspire us more than your forgiveness
      and nothing may dazzle us more than your beauty,
disclosed to us in your world, your story and your Son
Jesus Christ our Lord.
Amen.

2

Presiding genius?
Exciting the imagination

The priest as leader of worship

The title of the chapter is of course ironic. Not every priest is
a genius at leading worship, but they are all expected to be just
that. This is naturally something of a strain. Here in church
on a Sunday morning is a middle-aged woman looking for
worship which is both structured and beautiful to help her cope
with a life that is anything but. Here is an engaged couple who
have never been to church before and haven't a clue what to
do. Here is an English teacher who loves the cadences and
poetry of the Book of Common Prayer. At the back is a family
struggling with lively children, drawn to church through the
school, but not sure what they're looking for. Near the front
there's a couple in their fifties who have just been to a New
Wine Christian festival and want the enthusiasm quotient
moved up several gears. There's also an elderly woman who's
been bereaved recently, and a man who's registered blind
with his guide dog (whose worshipping needs are unclear).
This is the glorious, motley people of God, but how on earth
does the priest meet their needs in worship without turning
worship into either entertainment or therapy?

Worship looks first and last to God

It's important for the priest to remember that worship is a
profoundly simple movement of the heart offered in highly

complex situations. It's therefore even more necessary to be clear that worship is directed, first and foremost, towards God. We'll come back to other reference points later but fundamentally worship is for God, to God and of God. Worship is offering all of ourselves to all God has revealed himself to be, but it's about the Lord of heaven and earth before it's about us.

The priest understands that worship is the supreme expression of our humanity because it reminds us who we are in relation to who God is. The Westminster Confession said that 'the purpose of man [*sic*] is to worship God and to enjoy him for ever'. Worship is therefore a defining human activity. It's as basic to our being as thinking and working, reading and singing, laughing and playing. I worship, therefore I am. It's also very important for our emotional health. Worship is the means by which we interrupt our preoccupation with ourselves and attend to God. We're endlessly absorbed and fascinated with ourselves, our image and appeal. Worship is the great corrective to all this. It puts us back into a healthy relationship with ourselves, and with life, the universe and everything.

As the priest comes to prepare worship for next Sunday, therefore, he or she will need to be very clear that we are not dealing with a pitiful form of Christian entertainment. God is central. Worship is the lightning conductor through which God's life strikes the earth. It's exciting and dangerous to be mixing these divine and human chemicals together without being able to predict the outcome. Priests are meant to be able to handle this divine alchemy without blowing anyone up. It's not easy. Nor is public applause a significant measure of effectiveness.

In particular, worship exposes us to exhilarating encounters with both scripture and sacrament. Worship is a showcase for scripture and hearing the great story of God. It's also the occasion when earth and heaven come excitingly close in the sacramental meal of the eucharist. Here we sit at God's table, both re-entering the Upper Room and anticipating the final meal at the end of time. This meal is for many people the closest they come in this life to the halls of heaven, and it's the huge privilege of the priest to preside at this awesome occasion.

The high-octane potential of worship is linked to the level of our expectancy. It's interesting that we don't seem to pray '*maranatha*' (Lord Jesus, come) in our services very much these days, unlike the early Christians who were very keen in their longing for Christ to return. Is it because we think we've got life sorted, bar a few wrinkles? Leave it to us, Lord; we know what we're doing? Perhaps we need a much greater sense of expectancy in our worship. Sir Alec Guinness returned from church one day and met a lapsed Catholic friend who asked him: 'Had a nice Mass?' Sir Alec wanted to reply: 'Oh you know, the same old thing. The Real Presence at the altar, body, blood, soul, divinity of Christ, the usual.' God is both beautiful and terrifying, almighty love and a consuming fire. Our worship should be about nothing less.

Worship relates to the gathered people of God

If worship is first and foremost directed towards God, it relates, second, to the gathered people of God. The priest has the prime responsibility of presiding at an event that should help regular worshippers experience the healing re-alignment of self that good worship provides. Worship is the moment when we're both *broken open* and *repaired* at the same time. We're *broken open* to the majesty and love of God, to the beauty and angst of the world, and to the joyful detail of each other's lives. We're broken out of our self-enclosed, private worlds and placed on a bigger map and in a larger family. We can't truly encounter the living God and then go back to peeling the potatoes and cutting the lawn as if nothing had happened. At the same time, like a well-used piece of furniture, we're *repaired* by worship because the nails of our life and faith will often have worked loose during the week, and the glue will have come unstuck in places. What worship does is fit us together again, strengthening our joints and making us more 'serviceable' in God's work. This breaking open and repairing of our lives should be a normal consequence of worship, although people will articulate that process in many different ways.

A crucial, and worrying, question to ask of our worship, however, is whether people are indeed being led to an encounter with the profound and transforming reality of God. One city-wide study revealed that although there were many reasons why worshippers attended church, only 5 per cent of them believed they'd experienced anything they might call 'divine presence' on the particular Sunday they were interviewed. Moreover, 25 per cent of a sample of people who had stopped attending church gave as one of the main reasons the fact that they simply didn't feel they met God in the acts of worship in which they participated. When routine overtakes reality, and repetition replaces imagination, then worship is dying. A key question for worship leaders, therefore, is how, without manipulation, people are to be offered a context in which God may touch them and give them life. (Another question, of course, is whether people not only meet God, but also whether they meet each other in worship. Although much is made of the communal dimension of worship, there remains the suspicion that for many people worship is a solitary experience and community is what happens afterwards, over coffee, and not always even then.) Worship is shaped by the community in which it is offered and priests are those who have the responsibility of helping the worship to represent and express the life of the congregation. There's a strange synergy at work here and priests are in the middle of it.

The priest's competence in ordering worship is a crucial gift both to and from the people of God. The priest is dealing with their deepest needs and aspirations and helping them to offer the giftedness and complexity of their lives to God. The quality of our worship and the care and imagination we bring

After hours of rehearsal, the choir was ready to perform Messiah

to the task is therefore of the utmost significance. Anglicans are both helped and hindered by their service books. *Common Worship* seems in one sense to do it all for you. The liturgy, the different Eucharistic Prayers, the seasonal variations – it's all there in clarity and abundance. How then shall these bones live? That's where the skill and imagination of the priest is essential. How can the worship be both familiar and fresh each week? How can people be both reassured by the constancy of God and also stretched and surprised by God's originality? How can the worship represent the life of the community before God and allow God to re-present his grace to us?

Wise priests remember that they are the presidents, or presiders, at worship and not the celebrants. All the people of God celebrate the goodness and the mighty acts of God; the priest has the privilege of presiding at that community celebration. The priest will therefore, hopefully, recognize the huge resource of the congregation in planning worship. Others will bring not only their complementary views on what helps an act of worship to take wings and fly, but also particular gifts of music and drama, the ability to lead prayer imaginatively or to communicate with children, and so on. You may even turn up a lighting and soft-furnishings expert. Atmosphere is crucial, and can be helped by the arrangement of space, changes in lighting at different points of the service, the imaginative use of symbols, or the rare gift of silence. The ideas begin to flow when a group works together regularly on the whole experience of worship. The priest just needs to be unthreatened and to keep the group on course, shaping the ideas into living worship.

There is of course nothing so divisive as change in worship. I had the misfortune of becoming a footnote in ecclesiastical history when I supposedly dismissed the choir of the church I served. The details are unnecessary and would only tempt me to further self-justification. Suffice it to say that when the media smelled blood, the prey realized he'd underestimated the powerful forces that operate around music and choirs. National ignominy followed. However, the lesson I learned was that when conflict arises over such an important thing as worship 'jaw, jaw' is always better than 'war, war' and that the most useful strategy a priest can employ is to widen the discussion to encompass the various protagonists on some common ground. In my case we should have been discussing the nature of worship, its purpose, who it's for, complementary services and so on. The question then becomes: 'What can we unite on?' rather than 'What is it that divides us?'

Yet it is undeniable that the priest has to be at least competent and at best brilliant in the ordering of worship. Worship is the litmus test of our life as a church. It shows whether we are acidic or alkaline, alive or dead, whether we care deeply and passionately about God and each other or whether we are going through the motions and putting on what Peter Brook called 'deadly theatre'. It's the central responsibility of the priest. It may be the first question God asks us on the Last Day: 'Did you truly help to inspire my people to worship and to love?'

Worship relates to those who don't come to church regularly

Worship relates primarily to God, second to God's gathered people, and third to God's other people – those who don't come to church regularly, but might. In one sense we are already worshipping on their behalf. Not everyone will be in church but everyone can be represented. Those who worship regularly can be encouraged to see themselves as performing a service of profound value to the community by coming before God with praise and prayer on behalf of those whose imaginations have not yet been caught by the beauty of God.

Nevertheless, we can go further and recognize that in the course of a year a very large proportion of the population comes to church for one reason or another. In a recent poll 86 per cent of British people said they had been in a church in the past year. Moreover, over 40 per cent of people say they go to church for some event over the Christmas period. People come for baptisms (a huge turnout in most parts of the country, now that baptisms have taken over the social significance of weddings), for funerals, memorial services, carol services, school services, community thanksgivings and more. Here is a golden – or at least a silver – opportunity to present the positive, attractive face of the Church. The priest has an opportunity to deal well with people's experiences of transition and to show not only that the teaching of Christ offers profound wisdom on the vagaries of the human condition, but also that worship can be a powerful vehicle for a community's emotions and celebrations.

But here we have to be honest. The Church often succeeds wonderfully with such occasions, but on other occasions it's dire. Worship can both convert and repel. The conduct of worship can be incompetent, the music terrible, the Bible readings tired out, the sermon vacuous, and the whole experience empty. If everybody is on autopilot the occasional visitor to church may have his or her prejudices reinforced to the point of total resistance. Richard Harries, former Bishop of Oxford, wrote of a young man coming to church for the first time for many years. He was in many ways typical of his time – quite well off, relaxed, thoughtful, honest. He said he went to church with a sense of interest and expectancy but came away deeply disappointed. He felt diminished rather than enlarged, smaller and nastier rather than encouraged in a love of life and of other people. He probably never returned.

We need to offer worship that may suddenly resonate with the occasional attender and set up echoes of a far, forgotten land that needs investigating. It may mean subtle changes to regular services, or the addition of new services to meet the changing needs of our culture's 'secular children'. In either case the need is to enrich worship, to appeal to the senses, to use story and symbol and space and silence. One danger for us lies in making the assumption that there is a normative 'golden' age for liturgy (1662) or church music (nineteenth century) or preaching (Billy Graham). God's Spirit is constantly creative and we need the best of every age. Bring on the contemporary poets of the Word and artists of the Spirit!

'Fresh expressions' of church will draw out of its leaders, ordained and lay, an even wider range of liturgical experiment. An after-school Kids Klub needs another repertoire of worship resources and ideas that would leave the aficionado of 8 a.m. BCP Communion amazed – and hopefully delighted. Worship at a Youth Congregation or a small Alternative Worship community may use traditional ingredients such as visual stimuli, scripture, music and ritual but in forms hardly recognizable to a traditional church-goer. Café churches, network churches and churches based on community projects may hardly use 'worship' as usually understood at all, because they are more committed to exploration, experiment and personal experience as they build appropriate local communities. Priests working in these spheres need committed prayer and much encouragement.

In worship that looks to the needs of occasional attenders, therefore, the need is to use other languages of worship, other times for services, and other styles of exploration. In particular it will involve learning to handle informality with dignity. Now that's a priestly art! We need to be able to make worship natural before it can become supernatural, or it might end up being simply unnatural. The priest is the prime agent responsible, through the Holy Spirit, for whether the 'wow factor' is ever experienced in worship. It won't happen every time of course, but sometimes the priest might hope to hear people coming out of church saying: 'Wow, that was special!' or 'I'd come more often if services were like that' or 'I wonder what it is they've got?' Anything, rather than the Christmas greeting: 'See you next year then, vicar!'

Worship relates to the priest

The priest has to be aware of a great number of factors as he or she prepares worship during the week and then walks into church on Sunday morning. We've already looked at many of the issues: making sure worship focuses supremely on God, designing it to relate to the diverse needs of the gathered people of God but also to the occasional visitor. Moreover, there are scores of practical details behind any act of worship and the priest has to keep an eye on all of them in case the person responsible has forgotten what to do, failed to turn up, walked off in a huff, or fallen out with the church without you realizing it.

In the middle of all this the priest is also hoping to be able to worship God as another honest believer, and yet this may seem like just one thing too many to cope with. And that would be hugely disappointing to God, and also to the congregation, who actually can tell instinctively whether the priest is inwardly engaged with the worship or just going through the motions because of boredom, over-familiarity or a partial shut-down of the brain. So what can the priest do to enter the worship in as much spirit and truth as possible?

The first key is preparation of the heart. Leading worship is not just a technical skill; it's the bringing of the whole person before God in such a way that others are caught up in the drama and miracle of it all. However, practical preparation follows quickly on. If the priest knows precisely what should happen in the worship that he or she has prepared then the Spirit can transform the worship, smoke can fill the Temple, and burning coals can touch the lips of the preacher. If we are unprepared, everything will be on edge and no-one will be able to relax into the worship. I was once a visiting preacher and looked on aghast as the service appeared to be having a complete nervous breakdown. The parish priest had tried to sort out too many details at the last moment and it was chaos. Eventually he stood up and commanded the devil to leave! The chief sign that a service is well prepared is when the priest and others in leadership are able to go into quiet places in the chancel or sanctuary for some minutes before the start of the service, and pray.

The second key to the priest's own participation in the worship is the retention of a sense of awe and privilege *during the worship itself*. This is particularly the case with presiding at the eucharist. This is the service at the heart of our lives, where we re-inhabit the Passion of Christ and anticipate the Feast at the end of the world, and if ever we take it for granted then our priesthood has started to disintegrate.

The third key is attentiveness during the service, both to God and to the people's worship. This is an exhausting form of 'multi-tasking' and could and should leave us wrung out. But by this means we are entering fully into the reality of worship, representing the people before God and seeking to make God present to God's people. Nevertheless this isn't the same as being able to worship for oneself without carrying these responsibilities. It makes worship on holidays especially sweet (though also sometimes frustrating!).

The most common word for worship in the Greek New Testament is *proskuneo*, which means 'to come forward to kiss'. It's the exhausting joy and timeless privilege of the priest to be the 'presiding genius' as the Church leans forward to meet her Lord with such exquisite intimacy.

3

Spiritual explorer:
Passionately directed towards God

———•◆•———

The priest as person of prayer

He was clearly at the end of his tether. The priest with me was an able man, energetic, experienced and respected. He was a big man in every way, a brave thinker, an entrepreneur, and a man for whom prayer had been very important. But he was nearly burnt out. The spiritual tank was nearly empty and he had had the good sense to realize it. The way to advance was clearly to retreat. He needed to go on an eight-day retreat with an individual guide to accompany him on his spiritual journey back to base. He needed to go on a course focused on self-awareness in order for him to understand some of his habitual patterns of behaviour. And he needed a period quietly reading and thinking, away from the pressures of parish life.

He returned a different man. There was energy, sparkle and that mysterious but instantly recognizable quality called joy. He had got back in touch with that inner spring of life which had all but dried up. The water supply was back on. The colour was back in his life.

If priests are to be any use to anyone else they have to be passionate about God. God is our magnificent obsession. Like the bud of a sunflower following the sun throughout the day the priest has to be directed constantly towards God. That doesn't mean that the priest has to be good at it. Success and failure isn't the right language. It's the direction of gaze that matters. A wise spiritual guide said to me: 'Ask for the gift of prayer. The request is always granted. What follows is our prayer. It may not be what we expected or intended but it is "us" at prayer.'

There's no getting away from the absolute centrality of this hunger for God. What matters is that we long for God 'as in a dry and weary land where there is no water' (Psalm 63). It doesn't matter how we express it; if our devotion is more easily focused on Jesus Christ then it's Christ who has to fill our vision. 'It is no longer I who live but Christ who lives in me' (Galatians 2.20). 'For me, to live *is* Christ' (Philippians 1.21). It would be hard for Paul to have expressed it any more strongly.

So for the priest prayer is a matter of life or death. It's a tale of love and loss; it's an experience of joy and bewilderment; it's dancing and struggling with the divine lover. Sometimes it's sitting in the dark thinking that this is all folly. Sometimes it's all that life can hold. It's all part of the God-directedness of our lives. And it's irreplaceable.

Why am I being so insistent about this? Simply because, for the priest, when the passion is lost, shipwreck is only a matter of time. It's the stark truth that without God we cannot live; we can only take a longer or shorter time to die. The practice of ministry will often leave us feeling like a compass in a room full of strong magnets. Everywhere there are attractive possibilities into which we could put our energy, but one magnet above all must direct our life.

Moreover, people have a right to expect this from a priest. Certainly, we need to beware and resist the projections which can be placed on a priest – perfection in life, faith, prayer and the behaviour of our pets is hard to live up to – but they are right to expect the priest to be fascinated with the holy. If God is not the constant preoccupation of the priest how can anyone else be expected to take God seriously?

In a story from the desert fathers Abba Lot went one day to see Abba Joseph. He told him that he kept his rule of life as well as he could, including fasting and contemplation, prayer and meditation, and he tried to keep distractions at bay. What more could he do, he asked. Abba Joseph stood up to reply and raising his arms to heaven he said, 'Why not be totally changed into fire?'

The hidden life of prayer

Of course, in a sense, there can be no such thing as a hidden life of prayer for the priest. If it's not happening it will soon show! A famous pianist said that if he didn't practise for a day he noticed; if he didn't practise for two days his family noticed; and if he didn't practise for three days the public noticed. People will know if the priest is a person of prayer. Nevertheless, the priest is not to make a show of his or her prayer like the publican in Luke 8 who made sure everyone could see he was giving God the benefit of his attention. The priest needs to have a hidden life of prayer, and it's here that he or she patrols the borderland between earth and heaven, being at home in both, committed to the life of both.

Anglican clergy are bound by canon, and hopefully by choice, to a discipline of daily prayer in what is called the Daily Office – morning and evening prayer. This prayer works on us in quiet ways. It exposes us to scripture, psalms and spiritual songs (canticles) and it commits us to prayer as intercession. Essentially, however, it acts as a constant exposure to God and, just as the sea smooths the stone, so this exposure wears away the rough edges of our character and aligns us to the character of God. This is unspectacular prayer. Its function is to carry us and steady us, to hold us in times of turbulence and speed us onwards in times of high pleasure.

When I went to work in a cathedral I wondered how I would find choral evensong every day. I would have had a full day's work, dash in to evensong for 45 minutes, then back for a meal and straight out to an evening meeting. Would this be the prayer I needed to sustain me, I wondered. I discovered that it was precisely the prayer I needed. It carried me along in that great river of praise that's always making its way inexorably to the sea. For a few minutes I was carried along safely in my small boat. I didn't have to concentrate all the time (which was a good thing, because I didn't) but I was taken nonetheless and, best of all, my focus was re-directed towards God.

But the Office is not enough. It's a bedrock, and it's particularly valuable when a black frost envelops the soul, but by itself it's bread and butter without the jam and cream. Just like any other Christian – but particularly because our whole life depends on it – the priest needs time to be alone with God to let the boundaries of that relationship expand. This is not a book on prayer, and therefore this is not the time to write about different ways of praying, but the menu is vast. Each priest finds his or her own way, hopefully with a wise guide, and might explore, at different times, the possibilities of silence, Ignatian contemplation, lectio divina, imaginative prayer, symbols, icons, music, adoration, simple rest, and so on to the infinity of God. It's like breathing. If we grow breathless it's often a sign of heart trouble. Priests are in danger of heart trouble if they don't breathe deeply enough of the Spirit of God.

The importance of space and silence is hard to exaggerate. As a diocesan youth officer I was a committed activist, following youth culture avidly but maintaining only a twitchy spirituality. I was stopped in my tracks by a monk who declared to a group of us that without half an hour of silence each day we would burn out. Silence has since become indispensable to me, though sadly not often for half an hour a day. Many priests these days experience medically diagnosed stress at some time in their ministries. I'm no exception. There are many things to be done in such circumstances but one of them is the re-establishing of space and silence at the still centre of our dizzily turning world. Silence sifts and sorts our agitated hearts. It allows the sediment to drift to the bottom and leaves the spirit clear. But of course there are no rules. We pray as we are able, with the cherished liberty of the children of God. The one thing we can't do without, however, is the determination to pray.

The danger for one who prays professionally (as it were) is that we grow slack. Gradually the passion fades, routine takes over, expectancy withers. That's why a spiritual guide and companion is so necessary, why an annual retreat should go in the diary early on, and why days of reflection and quiet should punctuate the year. These are not luxuries. If the string on the bow grows slack, how can the arrow fly straight and true?

More profoundly, priests are almost bound at some stage to encounter periods of sheer emotional and spiritual weariness. Our forebears used to call it *accidie*. We've been turning the handle of parish life for years and it's all become unbearably heavy and unproductive. Prayer is a chore in the dark and a deep restlessness afflicts us. If this happens to us what matters is that we are honest with ourselves about what's happening and then seek help. Trundling on is one strategy but often a package of changes such as those made by the priest described at the start of this chapter will break the cycle of decline. This experience is more common than people imagine. It comes from handling the things of God for a long time and simply getting tired. No blame is attached and there are many classic descriptions of it. What matters is that we take it seriously but without getting too agitated. Relax – God has been here before!

The visible life of prayer

The priest's Daily Office may in practice be visible and not hidden prayer. It's a wonderful gift to priests if a small group of faithful Christians join them regularly in church to pray the Office. Many priests carry in their mental luggage the memory of George Herbert's Country Parson ringing the bell when the service was about to start and the workmen in the fields stopping and removing their caps, glad that their priest was praying for them. These days it's more likely that the ringing of the bell will prompt someone to take out an injunction to stop the sound pollution invading his country idyll. But we persevere.

How else does the priest make prayer visible? One way is the care with which he or she prays not only in church services but in PCCs and other meetings. Prayer on these occasions can all too easily seem like a perfunctory disinfecting of the meeting before the proper, adult work gets started, and therefore serious, imaginative praying can make a very significant difference to the atmosphere of the meeting. That doesn't mean using lots of prayers instead of a few. It means using few prayers well, making space for silence or short biddings from the group, or lighting a candle that stays lit for the whole meeting as a reminder that it takes place in the presence of the risen Christ. It means reflecting for two or three minutes on a verse of scripture – a Thought for the Meeting. It means being prepared to stop a significant discussion and pray silently for a few minutes to seek God's mind and wisdom. In other words, it means demonstrating that praying is a normal way for Christians to behave in all parts of their lives, not just the 'sacred' bits.

Priests will also make prayer visible by the way they pray comfortably and naturally with people on pastoral visits or after other ordinary conversations. The question being posed all the time by a priest's ministry is this: 'Is God a living reality or just a pleasant idea?' The priest's very appearance in the supermarket in a dog collar raises a question in people's minds: 'Do I believe what this person stands for?' In all sorts of ways in ministry the priest is making the claim that God is alive and well and living right here. Praying with people easily and openly is another part of the same fabric of witness. What the priest is saying is that God's presence is the most liberating reality of human experience, and the priest is inviting other people to live as if that is indeed true for them.

It also encourages others if priests can show that they are pilgrims too, and that they also struggle. No-one is really helped by an image (either true or created for impression) of a heroic priest, squeaky clean and shining with untroubled sanctity. Most people would just slink further into the shadows – including the bishop. We are all spiritual explorers; some have just been in the jungle longer than others. We all need each other's help and encouragement, so priests need to be honest too.

In these and many other ways priests can make prayer visible. Above all, they can pray regularly for the congregation and parish, and that steady, committed praying, tracking the rhythms and crises of the community, will mean more than anything, both to God and to his people. All those who know will be grateful – and some may even be tempted to join in.

The encouragement of prayer

Sometimes you go to a church where Sunday worship seems spiritually tepid. They're doing the right things but it's just not catching fire. The preacher's best lines seem to be hanging in the air looking for a home. The prayers bounce off the ceiling. The vicar's attempts to stoke up some enthusiasm are soaked up by apathy. One of the reasons for such a dispiriting phenomenon may be that people aren't praying during the week and therefore when they come to church on Sunday the spiritual temperature is starting from a very low point. Each week the worship has to get going from a standing start and it may take a full hour to get out of first gear.

A congregation needs encouragement to pray. One of the first things a priest may do in a new parish is to conduct an informal spiritual audit and try to discover where the spiritual fire is. It may be a particular service, perhaps even a midweek one; it may be a praying group or just a few praying individuals. But somewhere, if the church is alive spiritually at all, there will be a place where the fire is quietly burning. And that's the place to start.

Then we have to fan the flames. The hidden and visible prayer life of the priest will be a major influence on this. It's unavoidable that what the priest takes seriously, the congregation will ultimately take seriously as well. To some extent congregations grow into the likeness of their leaders. If the leader is committed to social action in the community, the church will probably become similarly committed. If the leader is enthusiastic about children's work or Taizé services or pilgrimages to Walsingham, the church may well come to reflect the same thing. So too with prayer. If it matters to the priest it will probably come to matter to the people. It's not automatic of course, but it's more than likely.

The priest can therefore make a point of preaching and teaching often about prayer and spirituality in a holistic and attractive way, making sure, for example, that prayer doesn't come across as only for introverts and ascetics. There can be retreats and quiet days, or a week of guided prayer. At certain times of year a short series can be offered on, say, silent prayer or Celtic prayer, on praying with icons or the Jesus prayer. The discoveries people make on such occasions can be exhilarating. Some introduction to a simple daily office could also be offered. In new forms of church the need and opportunity for experimentation is even greater. Suggestions from the group can be taken up and a liturgy created that allows for the bold use of atmosphere, symbol, scripture, image, space and silence. The pioneer priest needs great skill in negotiating the hunches of the group with the riches of the tradition, although it's interesting to note that many such groups are finding the need of some form of regular structured prayer or daily office.

The priest has the privilege of engaging in conversations that are out of the range of conventional expectation. If the priest has established a relationship of trust with the congregation it's possible to take some risks in pastoral encounters. I found in the parish that I could ask appropriate people, affectionately but seriously: 'So how's the prayer going, then?' The response indicated the level at which the person wanted to engage with the issue, but much more often than not such a question would lead into matters of moment. Here were opportunities for people to talk about deep and searching things, about aspirations and ideals, about darkness and bewilderment – if they wanted. And of course it made pastoral visits much more rewarding.

For many priests there is an ominous gap between the way they think they ought to be praying and the way they actually are praying. The gap is filled with guilt and feelings of failure. Jesus didn't scold his disciples about prayer. Indeed he operated more by example than by precept. But he did offer some memorable pictures as well. He told, for example, of the tax collector who collapsed in a heap saying only, 'God be merciful to me, a sinner,' comparing him favourably with the pharisee who had all the answers but none of the humility (Luke 18.9). What he valued in the tax collector, as in all his picture parables, was the direction of the heart. Which brings us back to the start of the chapter. What matters isn't what grades we would get in an A level Spirituality paper but where the heart is fixed. The crucial move to have made is the one that has surrendered to the Lord of Hosts. Sadly, experience suggests that there may be some priests who have simply not yet made that final surrender of the last high citadel of the heart – the last, carefully guarded, no-entry zone. When that citadel falls then it is at last, 'no longer I who live but Christ who lives in me'. Then we can say with the psalmist, 'my heart is fixed, O God, my heart is fixed.' And if the heart is fixed, then we can pray with joy, 'Abba . . .'

Gracious God,

you have given us the privilege of an open door to your presence.

When life is shining and full, inhabit our joy.

When life is grinding slowly on, touch us with your life.

When we long for a clearer vision of you, open our gauze-covered eyes.

When we studiously avoid your gaze, tempt us with your forgiving smile.

Lead us inexorably to the fulfilment of our lives in the service of your Son,

so that, dipped in God and cherished by your Spirit,

we may come to you, three times blessed,

Father, Son and Holy Spirit.

Amen.

4

Artful story-teller:
Opening up a world of grace

The priest as preacher

Every time I sit down to write a new sermon I go right back to the beginning. It's almost as if I've never preached before. Will I have anything to say? Will it make sense? How can I say anything worthwhile? Will they think 'He's finally lost it – if he ever had it'? Preaching is a vulnerable business. You're particularly exposed when you come down from the pulpit and you've given everything but you don't know whether the man on the fourth row with his eyes shut was merely concentrating, or fast asleep. I tell myself the time to start worrying is when I see people not just looking at their watches but rattling them to see if they're broken.

'I hate it when this happens,' said Toby

How often do people leave a service humming the sermon? It's an interesting test. How often are there ideas, insights, phrases, stories that people really want to hum all the way home? Sadly I reflect on the fact that each Sunday morning tens of thousands of sermons are preached in the churches of this country and most of them are instantly forgotten. Worse, many of them *should* be forgotten. Some of them are probably the source of considerable discomfort and boredom to faithful parishioners as matters of high and final significance are treated in a trivial or incompetent manner. It's a sign of the fundamental holiness of many congregations that they keep coming back week after week to sit through the preaching they're offered. I notice that a national newspaper said that a survey had shown that sermons were getting shorter and went on to suggest: 'this is an impressive testimony to the power of intercessory prayer.'

Priests are charged to 'proclaim the word of the Lord and to watch for the signs of God's new creation. . . . They are to unfold the Scriptures, to preach the word in season and out of season, and to declare the mighty acts of God' (The Ordinal 2005). It's a powerful calling. Thomas Carlyle once asked: 'Who, having been called to be a preacher, would stoop to be a king?' No wonder I feel daunted when I come to write a sermon!

The prayer I use at the start of my preaching is this: 'Father, may these *spoken* words be faithful to the *written* word and lead us to the *living* Word, Jesus Christ our Lord.' I use that prayer because that's what I believe preaching is about.

These spoken words

Spoken words are all we've got. Ordinary, everyday words. And somehow we have to craft them so that they carry the weight of eternal possibilities. Words are often used carelessly in our culture. T. S. Eliot wrote of the 'sleet and hail of verbal imprecision'. We spray words around indiscriminately, using ten words when two would do. Priests do it too – someone once spoke of the clergy's 'fatal facility for continuous utterance'. Another said of the clergy that they are like old shoes – the tongue is the last bit to wear out!

We need to use words with care and respect. This means they need to meet many criteria. They need to be vivid and alive, more verbs than nouns. They need to be visual, using images that stay in the memory because our minds are more like art galleries than libraries. They need to tell stories because stories are the common language of every culture, the discourse that we use with children as they first encounter the world, and with old people as they finally leave it, the normal currency of television soaps, films, novels, celebrity magazines, TV news reports, even adverts. We need not to be afraid of humour, because humour is part of the deep structure of our humanity, and to exclude it from our preaching is therefore to 'de-humanize' our worship – a common-enough accusation anyway.

There are no rules about preparing sermons except to make sure that we do it. Some priests 'economize' on preparation, justifying it on the grounds of lack of time or a preference to be up-to-the-minute and spontaneous, responding to the word of God from the heart. The consequence, in most cases, is preaching of poor quality, leaving the congregation short-changed or insulted. On the other hand some of the most brilliant preachers I know go into the pulpit with barely a note. They have read around the sermon, mulled and prayed over it, worked out a clear structure, and delivered it in the study, but they know that they communicate best when they are free of notes. Nevertheless the preparation has not been 'left to the Holy Spirit' – a nice-sounding excuse which shouldn't convince anybody!

The priest has to take seriously the multiple changes that have taken place in our culture and the different ways that people are now accustomed to taking in information and making connections. People are used to low-key communication, informal chat-shows, late-night discussion programmes, consultation, participation. They're uncomfortable with authoritative communication from one person to an obedient crowd. It may be, therefore, that on some occasions, and in particular in some of our fresh expressions of church, a different format is required – interviews, talks delivered in two or three slots, data-projection with quotes and film-clips to reinforce and enrich the message. By whatever means 'proclaim the message, in season and out of season' (2 Timothy 4.2).

In order to check our words and see if any of them have found a home anywhere, it can be a very good practice to build in a feedback mechanism. This is done by asking some people we trust to give us honest feedback on our sermons. We give them permission to say the hard things but we ask for a balanced assessment, strengths and weaknesses, because we seriously want to improve. Without some form of quality control we may repeat the same errors, omissions and irritations all our ministry. Spouses are usually not the best candidates for this role for reasons of family harmony!

Faithful to the written Word

The check on the priest's indiscriminate use of poorly prepared words is his or her faithfulness to the written Word as contained in scripture. The Bible is our touchstone, our authority and our basic raw material. I once knew a priest who was delightful, but would often start a sermon by saying he'd like to 'share a few thoughts' about, say, the resurrection. I can't imagine that 'sharing a few thoughts' is what St Paul had in mind when he said: 'Woe betide me if I do not proclaim the gospel' (1 Corinthians 9.16).

The theologian D. T. Niles said that the Bible is 'food for wrestlers'. As preachers, priests are called to wrestle with the Bible, to engage in strenuous conversations with it and so engage God's wisdom with the concerns of our life and times.

Preachers have before them the great narrative of God, the story that tells us where we are and why we are, the story that our culture is in danger of forgetting. We need to come to this extraordinary living text with all our faculties engaged but with proper humility. We aren't there to judge the Bible from the superiority of our post-modern world-view which is suspicious of all metanarratives; we're there to listen, to struggle, to wrestle, and to learn, because the preacher is under the authority and judgement of the text as it mediates the authority of God.

The preacher's task is to discover the heart of the message of the text that day. This requires the skill of 'double listening' – attending to the word of scripture and to the life of the world. Finding that distillation of the message is the single most difficult and vital part of the process of preparing a sermon, but until it's done the preacher had better not go any further. There will be trouble down the line if we do. When I have been most in despair over a sermon late on a Saturday night and most likely to tear it up and start again, it's usually because I've not been absolutely sure what I've been trying to say. Is it so clear that I could put it in a sentence or two and say it confidently (though perhaps somewhat differently) to the tutor who taught me New Testament and to a child in Junior Church?

The priest's challenge as an artful story-teller is to find ways of communicating this crock of gold (which by now he or she believes it to be) so that the congregation is deeply engaged and, indeed, excited by the gospel. It's important to capture the imagination of the congregation from the start and to build a movement or process into the sermon so that the congregation is taken through the whole drama. There are of course many ways of structuring a sermon and this isn't the place to explore them. However, one way is for the preacher to set up an initial problem that society faces or a human dilemma common to many of the congregation. The next step is to explore that dilemma further, to deepen and thicken the plot, illustrating it from various sources, particularly contemporary and topical ones. Then comes the crucial move which Tolkien calls the 'eucatastrophe', the moment of overturning, where the gospel addresses the dilemma, re-frames it, and in some significant way transforms it. The sermon then works out some of the applications of this radical gospel change, and leaves the congregation to go and get on with it. What the congregation has been through is a whole series of homiletic 'moves' that have pivoted around the words of scripture. It's been well said that the preacher's task is not to explain the gospel but to evoke the gospel and to invite people to become part of the gospel story. The goal isn't information but transformation through an encounter with the One who stands behind the story.

We ought never to forget that the gospel has come to us predominantly in narrative form and that the deep structure of our lives is also narrative in shape. Everything is set up, therefore, for the preacher to find ways of fusing the two so that people's lives might, by God's grace, be transformed. We're called to the demanding task of artful story-telling – but we've been given all the aces, in particular the extraordinary story of Jesus and of people's encounters with him through history. Narrative is a key category for the preacher. People remember stories because we all live in a sea of them. Jesus understood this very well and constantly told stories out of contemporary experience. Nor did he feel the need to be apologetic about them, as some preachers do today. Stories, well told, to the point, and avoiding sentimentality (but not avoiding humour) are some of our richest resources.

Lead us to the living Word

For any preacher, including the priest, just as the test of our use of *words* is our faithfulness to scripture, so the test of our use of *scripture* is whether it leads to Christ himself. All truly Christian communication leads to an encounter, in some form, with the living Christ. So the priest will want to ask the question: 'Does my preaching lead people to Christ – or is it a sharing of my own pet ideas and prejudices?' This doesn't mean, of course, that each sermon is a call to repentance and faith. What it means is that Christ is the template of our preaching, often the shape, and always the goal.

A theological student once went to his tutor with a copy of the sermon he was going to preach and asked anxiously: 'Will it do?' The tutor answered: 'Will it do? Will it do *what*?' Precisely. What will our sermons do? Will they lead people to the living Word, the luminous figure of Jesus Christ? When the priest has laboured over the text, the theology, the context, the right images, the stories, the best use of words – still the question remains: could this sermon lead people to Christ and the possibility of some form of transformation?

One acid test of the priest's preaching is whether what he or she has written is gospel or law. I've had many seminal moments in my thinking about preaching. One was a church-warden's wife telling me that in her experience no priest ever had more than seven basic sermons which they preached over and over again. Another was someone reflecting that most sermons ended up saying some form of 'love more, come to church more, or give more time and money'. Any conclusion that begins 'So, let us . . .' is likely to be an exhortation which leaves the congregation in the realm of law rather than gospel with more demands being made of the hapless Christian. If a sermon is gospel, on the other hand, it will lead us to a new exposure to the glorious liberty of the children of God. There will be a new encounter with the reckless, unconditional love of God, a new experience of the breath-taking, gravity-defying scale and beauty of God. This in turn may then lead to new undertakings in discipleship but these new commitments are never a prerequisite of the gospel of grace that we preach.

There's a sting in the tail of any of our thinking about the priest as preacher and it is this. The priest will never be an effective preacher if his or her life isn't congruent with the graceful story he or she is trying to tell. Are we embodying the gospel life? Because if we aren't there will be a severe case of spiritual dissonance. As a small child, one of our daughters was in strong disagreement with us at the tea table. We were saying we loved her, completely, and she was hotly denying it. The argument continued for quite a while until eventually she stormed off from the table declaring to me forcefully: 'You shouldn't lie. You're a man of God.' To her, at that moment, the spiritual dissonance had become too great!

The sharp truth is that, for many people, the life of the priest is the only 'holy book' they will ever read. Forget about lesser failings like watching *Neighbours* or supporting Chelsea; those are mistakes, not really sins. But the whole shape and direction of our lives can't be disguised. People in a real sense 'see through us' as priests and either they see Jesus or they see something much less attractive. If we are preaching Christ we need to live lives that are faithful to the graceful ways of Christ. If we're trying to lead people to the burning bush we have to be walking on the holy mountain ourselves.

I have one piece of comfort. Actually, two. The first is the wisdom of the theologian Helmut Thielicke who once said that all good sermons are heresy. The reason of course is that all good sermons will make one good point so well that other truths have to be side-lined. You can't preach everything all the time. We need to find the one pearl that we believe is God's gift for this congregation at this time. It's a single pearl, a discrete gift, but it's worth a Kingdom.

The other truth is this: when we're preparing sermons faith tells us we never work alone. Every sermon offered to God with openness and integrity is co-written by the Holy Spirit. He doesn't let us off the hook in terms of preparation but he shares the load and provides the inspiration. Then our spoken words may indeed be faithful to the written word and lead us to the living Word, even Jesus Christ himself.

5

Multilingual interpreter:
Exploring the landscape of faith

————◆◆◆————

The priest as apologist

'So how do you answer that? How can someone believe in God when tens of thousands of people die in such a horrific earthquake?' I was sitting in a local radio studio reviewing the newspapers on the morning show. A woman had phoned in to protest about belief in God and I had to find the bite-sized answer which was all time would allow. Another occasion: 'Bishop, why is the Church so nasty to gays?' Or again: 'Don't you find it dispiriting that the Church is on its way out? To young people it's just naff.'

Hard questions are the stuff of the front line, and even if they're not articulated, they're always in the air. The priest is the most visible symbol of the Church, and the most vulnerable. He or she has to be able to handle the tough questions. It's the role of the apologist.

The pastoral imperative

The most obvious place where the priest encounters a spoken or unspoken challenge to faith is at a funeral. As C. S. Lewis put it: 'Every tombstone is a monument to unanswered prayer.' Of course, a funeral is also the least appropriate place for an apologetic *tour de force*. The sickbed, the bereavement visit and the funeral service need intense sensitivity from the priest as he or she tries to match the moment with an appropriate response. The underlying questions may not require any kind of reasoned answer at that particular point but the deeper need remains, as demonstrated by the ingrained responses to tragedy that so often emerge: 'I don't know what he did to deserve this', or 'God must have taken him for a reason'.

Listening to people going through the kind of dark valleys that we may not even be able to imagine teaches us humility and the importance of silence, but it doesn't obviate the need for a priest to be able to offer some reference points at the appropriate time. The priest is an apologist as part of being a pastor. Giving people a more mature framework of interpretation for their hard experiences is part of helping someone to grow and to live more wisely.

The need to be able to defend and commend the faith (a good definition of apologetics) is provided by other pastoral encounters too. Baptism preparation elicits all kinds of strange ideas about God and the Church, as may chance conversations with the postman, the local MP or even the churchwarden. In a previous existence the priest could avoid these forays into disputed territory with a laugh, a throwaway remark or a promise to ask the vicar. Now, however, you *are* the vicar and you are the one who has to make the response. And you have to judge whether the invitation to respond is a serious one, at what level to answer it, what language to use, and whether you are equipped to answer in any case. This apologetic discernment is not a straightforward matter but the priest is the one who carries the responsibility. Clearly there is a particular sharpness to this apologetic role for sector ministers and ministers in secular employment. They are operating in secular territory without the normal polite conventions that usually still accompany the work of the parish priest. Such ministers have important lessons to teach the rest of the Church about the challenges that the (post-)secular world is throwing down.

As ever, one of the best ways to improve our pastoral and apologetic effectiveness is to review conversations after they've happened. What was really going on there? What was she really asking? Did I ask the most appropriate questions to clarify the issue? Did that response seem to help her at all? What might I have said differently? Another way is to listen to bishops being interviewed on the morning show and ask how you would have handled it better!

The young people imperative

The number of young people attending church has halved in the last 25 years. To very many young people 'religion' is a dirty word and professing dislike for it is almost a social necessity. Belief in God is deemed intellectually indefensible, and Christians are seen as having swallowed an unreconstructed package of beliefs that require unquestioning obedience. Churches, in the meantime, are cold, unwelcoming and out of touch, and it's assumed that the Christians in them are hypocrites. The old morality is dead, based as it is on negativity and repression; the new morality, meanwhile, puts the highest value on tolerance and freedom of choice.

None of this is encouraging to the priest as an apologist. Indeed, working with young people – whose freedom of expression is legendary – is often the area where the priest feels most vulnerable. Nevertheless it's an area of witness that pays huge dividends when put into the wider framework of growing the Kingdom slowly and faithfully. Our young people not only have infinite value in their own right, they will also be the adult citizens who constitute society in the future. If they've dismissed the Church's message now, the ground will be that much harder in 20 years' time. But the evidence is that young people's critique of the Church and its faith is often effectively subverted when they actually encounter good, credible, Christian witnesses. The abstract 'religious person' is a projection that has to be undermined and there's no way of doing that except by personal encounter. Whether that encounter is in school RE lessons, in youth activities or at bus shelters, it's worth the effort. Sometimes it's exhilarating when an exchange is honest and personal. Young people give so much of themselves when they feel safe. My memory of youth work and being a Diocesan Youth Officer is that these times were some of the most rewarding (and frustrating) of my life.

What ultimately convinces people of the value of faith is when they see it at work in someone's life. Rarely does a set of intellectual answers bring someone to faith. But when young people encounter a priest or another Christian living their faith with integrity, courage and obvious enjoyment, a process is started which opens up the possibility of a different interpretation of life which might eventually be a route to faith. But young people are also very quick to pick up lack of authenticity. As ever, the priest is a 'walking sacrament' and the quality of Christlikeness is the mysterious *sine qua non* which no-one can fake and which grows from within by continual exposure to God. Then my best advice to a priest is to pray hard, to be confident in Christ, and then to get involved – with a team of good people alongside.

The cultural imperative

A young research scientist with an engaging personality and an open mind went through a Christian basics course with interest and commitment. At the end, however, he said with some regret that he couldn't embrace the Christian faith because 'the world simply isn't like that'. He clearly had a spiritual side to his nature – he was no reductionist – but the way that Christianity configures the world was simply not credible to him. This is the kind of response that sends a chill down the spine of the priest. It illustrates the distance that our culture has drifted away from its Christian roots, or the inability of the Church to speak in a language the ordinary intelligent person grasps. To many good, thoughtful people Christianity just doesn't make sense. It isn't a matter for blame, more for sorrow, but it needs to be taken with the utmost seriousness. Social scientists talk about a paradigm shift in our whole Western world-view, our values, structures and institutions. In a few short generations there's a new world, such that people born now cannot even imagine the world into which their grand-parents were born. This new post-modern landscape has been too well documented to need rehearsing here but the implications for the Church and the role of the priest are profound.

The Church is caught up in this deep structural shift. No priest can afford to keep doing the same things in the same way as they were done in the 1970s. We have a culture where all meta-narratives are suspected of being power-plays, where you make your own choices and construct your own reality, where you channel-hop and surf the net to engage with the surface con-tours of our culture but you move on before getting too deep. This last characteristic is particularly confusing to traditional forms of church where the potent images are of 'depth' and 'foundations' rather than 'surface' and 'speed'. The danger is that Christians could become cultural exiles in a society where we now find bookshops placing the Bible in the section marked 'Esoteric' – and this in a culture shaped at its deepest level by the Christian faith.

When faced with this relentless suspicion, antagonism and apathy to the faith that they hold dear it's important for priests not to lose their nerve. One of our fundamental theological convictions is that men and women are made in the image of God, are endlessly loved by him, and will find their fulfilment supremely in him. No matter what they think of Jesus, Jesus thinks that they are worth his life, and the priest is an agent of that inexhaustible love. Confident in that truth, the priest goes out to engage with the prevailing culture thoughtfully and gracefully, and on issues of real and lasting concern. Broadly these will be *pre-modern* questions to do with meaning and purpose, *modern* questions to do with truth and reality, and *post-modern* questions to do with practical living and life-style.

The *pre-modern questions* don't change. They may be differently framed today but questions about the meaning or meaninglessness of life, and about the origin and destiny of the universe and of us within it, are always being asked. Priests need to have a clear theological map so that they can move around the various 'grid points' in order to offer cogent, faith-based interpretations. This means continuing our theological reading rather than letting our theology be a hardened deposit of truth that becomes more and more inaccessible the further away we get from our original training. It also means being able to make our explanations in both *Daily Mirror* and *Guardian* language, depending on the need.

Modern questions about truth shouldn't be ignored just because they are out of favour. The problem otherwise is that people will assume that these issues have simply been resolved, and not in God's favour. It will be assumed that agnosticism is the obvious mark of a sound, rational and healthy mind, that Jesus couldn't possibly be more than another good prophet, that science and religion are in permanent conflict, and that religion is at the root of most of the world's problems. And if there's still any doubt, suffering is the final proof either that God doesn't exist or that he's culpably negligent. The priest needs to be able to make credible responses to these assumptions, which are all the more insidious for being taken as given. We need to be prepared to say as often as necessary: 'Actually, I'd like to go back and re-visit the assumptions I think are being made here . . .'

Post-modern questions about the practicalities of living, making choices and living well make up another whole raft of issues for the priest to be engaged with. This is where ethical issues come to the fore and where the current fascination with spirituality is an important, if frustrating, arena of dialogue. Spirituality is clearly very popular today. It usually seems to have a somewhat Eastern flavour and is associated with wisdom, experience, mysticism and self-help. Spirituality is contrasted favourably with religion in a clear stand-off. Spirituality is seen to be about freedom, and religion about control; spirituality is open, and religion is narrow-minded; spirituality is accepting, and religion is judgemental. The priest has to understand the depth of this dichotomy in order to face it seriously, while also recognizing that people's fascination with spirituality may be a hunger for the holy which Christian faith is well able to address if offered sensitively and intelligently.

Preparing to be an apologist

What resources, then, can help the priest to deal with the ambiguities of a post-modern culture? This is where the skills of 'double-listening' become so important. We have to listen to the *tradition* (Bible and Church) in order to recognize the deeper echoes of today's idolatries. (More of that in the next chapter.) We also have to listen to the *culture* in order to read the signs of the times. Reading a Sunday newspaper and its colour supplements gives a fascinating insight into alternative life-styles. Films are a powerful cultural influence and we can benefit from seeing some of them and reflecting on what they are saying. Many priests find it helpful to know what's happening in the television soaps and what they tell us about how people are thinking. Modern novels give us access to world-views we wouldn't otherwise experience. A study of adverts and the cult of celebrity, and how sport acts as a quasi-religion in the lives of millions of younger men, and why *The Da Vinci Code* was such a massive success – all these feed our understanding. They represent important sources of information – and many are enjoyable too – but our culture is now so complex that 'getting a flavour' is probably all that is possible, and trying to 'keep up' in a comprehensive way is now doomed to failure.

The awareness we gain from swimming in this post-modern sea (always trying to keep our head above water) needs to fuel our preaching, teaching, conversation, evangelism, youth

On the pancake, as if by a miracle, was the face of Gary Lineker

and children's work, and much else. But the priest needs to be careful. He or she needs to be courteous and generous in conversation, not dogmatic and aggressive. We need to listen to make sure we've understood what's being said, and we need to *offer* our own interpretation rather than to *insist* on it. If we have an attitude of open exploration in a conversation that's full of grace it will be much more effective than trying to persuade a reluctant victim or argue them into the ground. Ultimately, people are motivated more by their imaginations, emotions and desires than by their intellects, and how we reflect the beauty of God will prove more influential than our rational arguments.

When I was young and over-zealous I once got into a discussion with my atheist grandmother about the resurrection. With argument after argument I gradually beat her down until eventually she conceded. 'You may have won the argument,' she said, 'but you'll never convince me.' I felt ashamed. I'd won a battle and lost a war. And I'd tried to pin a free spirit to the ground to prove the superiority of my faith or, more likely, my own intellect.

One last thing: there's no need for priests to become too intense about this apologetic task. God is actually quite big enough to look after himself. It's better for us to engage with others from the basis of an expansive, joyful faith than as worried defenders of God's dignity. A similar point might be made to the professional Christian protesters who take up arms against every affront to their faith. I don't think God gets too indignant about these things; he's seen it all before and he still believes in us.

Priests are multilingual interpreters. They interpret the faith to the wider culture, and the culture to the faith community. It's a fascinating and demanding task that puts them on the front line of mission every day, particularly the priest whose main ministerial arena is the workplace. Above all it asks priests regularly to put their faith up for scrutiny, to give a reason for the hope that's in them (1 Peter 3.15).

And that can't be a bad thing for a Christian disciple who's always learning.

6

Inquisitive learner:
Digging into theology

The priest as theologian

When I'm interviewing priests for new posts I like to ask three key questions. The first is, 'What is the Christian gospel to you? In other words, what's good about the Good News? People in the parish will hear you say it in a hundred different ways, but what essentially will they hear as the heart of your message?' The second question is this: 'How do you sustain yourself spiritually? What are the different wells you draw from?' And the third is, 'How do you feed yourself theologically? What do you read? What courses do you go on?'

If prospective candidates have a gospel to share, a life of prayer to sustain them, and an enquiring mind to equip them, then they might well be right for the post. Sadly, however, it's on the last question that I most often find myself wanting to help a luckless candidate who can't remember the name of any book he or she has read in the last year. I have the same sinking feeling when I visit a priest's study and find the range of books limited to those in vogue when he or she was training. There may be the odd beguiling paperback next to a recent liturgical resource but nothing to set the theological pulses racing. Nevertheless I fully accept the charge that could be made against others of us who have many new books on our shelves – most of them unread!

We would be unlikely to be impressed if our doctor told us he didn't have time to do any medical reading these days, and he gave up the *British Medical Journal* years ago. We want our medical advisers to be on the ball, and the same is true of our spiritual advisers. Our theology was not given us to place in a bank vault, only to be brought out in extreme circumstances and rarely replenished. In the current jargon, we are called to be 'life-long learners', or, in the words of the ordination service, to be 'of godly life and sound learning'. At a time when some priests are anxious about what remains distinctive about their ministry when so much is now shared with other people in the parish, here is a crucial role for priests; they are the trained, 'professional' theologians of the congregation, and, as the Church has found throughout its life, if the theology fails, the local church often goes off the rails.

Of course all the people of God are theologians. We all have a working theology which may or may not be articulated in systematic ways but is nevertheless effectively the basis of our prayers and our discipleship. Readers, local preachers and other lay theologians are also trained in biblical, liturgical, ethical and other disciplines. We always need to work collaboratively in ministry. However, the unique gift and calling of the clergy is that they have a duty to carry this responsibility and to encourage other theological voices. Others may; clergy must.

The priest as a practical theologian

The special calling of a priest is to be a practical theologian, revealing and clarifying the connections between the things of God and the things of people's everyday experience. In some cases the connections are obvious and urgent. The death of a child leads us to reflect on suffering and theodicy; starting a healing ministry leads us to reflect on divine action; the invasion of a country in the Middle East leads us to re-examine just-war theory; a new book by Richard Dawkins leads us to think about science and religion. At other times the connections are less pressing but they're the material out of which maturity of faith grows. How do we reflect theologically on the closure of a local factory, a Government White Paper on education, a cult television programme, or a national sporting triumph? How do we help people to connect their thinking about God to their life at work, their ambitions and decisions in the workplace, the bringing up of their children, or the care of their father-in-law with dementia? Only connect.

The skills priests need are those of practical theologians, who take the 'text' of human lives and actions as the raw material of doing theology, and help others to be more skilled at making connections between the Word and the world. It means taking the ordinary stuff of life with proper seriousness and enjoying the depth of events and the rich hinterland behind daily happenings. The key question beloved of practical theologians is always, 'Where is God in all this?', which might lead on to asking, 'What's the most godly action we could take here?' and later, perhaps, 'How could we pray about this?'

The first question, about what God is up to in the heart of some human event or experience, is the crucial one, and one of the most helpful tools the priest has here is the pastoral cycle he or she will have encountered in training. There are other processes, of course, from a contextual reading of the Bible to prayerful reflection, but the pastoral cycle is a good basic approach. In ministry we're always starting with fascinating *experiences* which cry out for deeper understanding. As Rowan Williams says, we are always starting in the middle of things. This leads on to further *exploration*, using other skills or disciplines that allow us to examine the historical, sociological or psychological information that seems relevant here. This in turn takes us to the key move of *reflection* using all the theological tools available in scripture and the tradition. And that process takes us to new possibilities of graceful *response* to the original situation, and to the next turn of the cycle.

The pastoral cycle is well proven as a way of thinking theologically about ministry; the trouble is that it's a pain to do! If it has to be an intentional, solitary activity for the hard-pressed priest faced with yet another pastoral demand, it's not surprising if it fails to excite the priest's imagination. This way of thinking must either be undertaken corporately with colleagues or become an instinctive part of the way a priest works – or both. It won't inspire many priests as a deliberate, mechanical series of steps but only as a natural, thoughtful response to the eventfulness of ministry. If this kind of theological reflection becomes a natural way of thinking (preferably with others) it helps a priest's ministry avoid becoming a series of knee-jerk reactions that simply repeat a limited number of 'off-the-shelf' ministerial responses. The priest will always be on the move intellectually (even if slowly!), building on previous experience and integrating all the inputs and variables of ministry. This theological connectivity makes the life and work of a priest a fascinating ministerial gavotte with God – if we can keep up with him – and with others. The important point of course is that we'll only *think* theologically if we're *feeding our minds* theologically.

Specialist subjects

Some priests will happily commit themselves to continuing study in a specific discipline or around a specific subject. They are then likely to be used as tutors in Reader training, education for discipleship courses and ministerial training schemes. This is both valuable for the courses and refreshing for the priests. It varies the priestly diet and keeps turning over the theological soil. It also subverts the unhealthy split that easily recurs between the parish and the academy. The tradition of the scholar-priest might be difficult to maintain among the massive demands of contemporary ministry, but hopefully it won't be relinquished entirely. It needs to take different forms today. Not many parish priests will be writing cutting-edge theology, but many will be contributing to the intellectual life of the diocese in their roles in teaching, training and supervising. More and more students for ordained or lay ministries are looking for supervised placements and having such a student can be enlivening for both priest and parish. Supervision is itself a skilled art and a fascinating process. There's also need for mentors, senior friends, ministry consultants, mission accompaniers and more. In other words, there's enough work for everybody!

Sixth-day ministries

Another form of intellectual vitality can be released by the encouragement of every priest to have a 'sixth-day ministry'. This is an area of interest in ministry which is genuinely life-enhancing for the priest, and potentially valuable for the wider Church. He or she might have developed an interest or expertise in the environment, Godly Play, creative writing, Celtic spirituality, the Orthodox Church, leading retreats, urban theology, Taizé, alternative worship, fresh expressions of church, overseas links, film and faith, internet evangelism, or a hundred other interests. It's a constant source of joyful amazement to me to discover the range of wild and wonderful interests that people have. The Church should let them thrive. This would mean encouraging priests to pursue those interests, and to seek further expertise through courses and memberships, and then to offer their enthusiasm to the wider Church at deanery, diocesan or even national level. This has the dual advantage both of benefiting the Church and also giving priests permission to use an enthusiasm as a gift to themselves and to others. Five days are for the parish or other priestly task, the sixth day is for the specialism.

Having made a case for these specialist ministries, however, I also want to affirm the distinctive specialism of the priest as a generalist. There are few people in society today who have at the heart of their role the task of holding disparate things together. Understandably society has gone down the path of increased specialization with people knowing more and more about less and less. Parish priests on the other hand are expected to think holistically about the health and well-being of a community. They have to keep examining the big picture in the light of a multitude of details. Priests specialize in being generalists, in holding together the complexities of a community's life and seeing it in the light of God's purposes. The priest pops up everywhere because nothing is outside God's interest, and God's vision for our flourishing is always more inclusive and breath-taking than we have ever imagined.

Resources for theological refreshment

How, then, will hard-pressed priests find their theological energy renewed? The fact is that there has never been more opportunity. My father was a priest and he died at 83. When he was 80 he was still buying commentaries using the Greek text. There's no shortage of books; it's only the will that's required – and the money! However, there's also an abundance of intermediate books that busy priests could enjoy, neither too heavy-duty nor too frivolous. Moreover, there has never been a time when we have had more courses, conferences and opportunities to travel, especially on sabbatical, which ought to be taken every seven or ten years to allow for rest, spiritual refreshment, and a theological or ministerial focus of study.

In particular we have available today a plethora of academic programmes at Masters or Doctoral level which not only enable the priest to renew his or her academic muscles but also refresh the whole person. As long as the level is right and the demands are not counter-productive, undertaking an MA, for example, can renew a priest's ministry both mentally and spiritually. I started an M.Litt. when I was 40 and relished the chance to discover what I'd forgotten, what I never knew, and what I didn't realize I never knew! The effect for me was truly transformational. Of course not every priest finds academic work fun or even a stimulus. Some reflection is best done sitting by a river and pondering. Some is done on our knees. Some is done as we watch a group of children at play.

However, some of the richest resources for theological refreshment are our colleagues. Priests generically (and in a brave generalization) have a serious need to get past their fear and rivalry in relation to their colleagues. There can be a tendency in clergy meetings to interact by way of provocative statements rather than by appreciative listening. We need instead to be able to enjoy each other's company both personally and theologically. The questions we need to address to each other are: 'What do you think?', 'How do you approach this issue?', 'Have you read anything about this recently?' Then we can benefit from each other's theology and practice, and we may even find that the colleague we are most threatened by is one of God's greatest resources to us. But all our colleagues and lay people are rich in experience and wisdom; we just need to value it.

Each Tuesday morning in one of the parishes I served we had our staff meeting. We would start, coffee mugs in hand, by looking at next week's Gospel reading, each person offering some immediate reflection on what it meant to him or her. Having gone round the circle, we would let the conversation run, seeing which were the live issues, theologically, personally and spiritually. For 30 or 40 minutes we met around scripture in a way that opened us up to each other, gave us new insights, fed our minds and hearts, integrated our ministries, and possibly gave us some clues for next week's sermon. It was time very well spent. We were glad to be theologians of the local church, equipping each other for the task we were privileged to share with others but for which we had a particular vocation and responsibility. I think we remained 'inquisitive learners' in the Lord's school of discipleship. I hope we always will.

Part Two

THE PAIN OF
THE WORLD

——■◆◀■——

O God,
it is your will to hold the world in a single peace.
May the generous authority of your love
shine on the fractures and sorrows of the nations
and the wounds of your people
and so bring healing to our politics
              healing to our neighbourhoods
              healing to our families
              and healing to our hearts,
through Jesus Christ our Lord.
Amen.

7

Pain bearer:
Keeping vigil with a damaged world

The priest as intercessor

There is a huge amount of pain washing around in any community, and one of the more difficult – but often more rewarding – roles of a priest is to bear the pain with others and hopefully, in some way, to move it on. It's rare that a priest's ministry can actually take the pain away, but it's certainly possible to loosen the icy grip of the pain and perhaps to move it into a different relationship to its victim. But the priest may be the one who, quite personally, carries the burden and pays the price.

This of course can be the gift of all Christians through their common priesthood. In his book *The Go-Between God* John V. Taylor writes movingly of one such pain-bearing encounter:

A West Indian woman in a London flat was told of her husband's death in a street accident. The shock of grief stunned her like a blow, she sank into a corner of the sofa and sat there rigid and unhearing. For a long time her terrible tranced look continued to embarrass the family, friends and officials who came and went. Then the school-teacher of one of her children, an Englishwoman, called and, seeing how things were, went and sat beside her. Without a word she threw an arm around the tight shoulders, clasping them with her full strength. The white cheek was thrust hard against the brown. Then as the unrelenting pain seeped through to her the newcomer's tears began to flow, falling on their two hands linked in the woman's lap. For a long time that is all that happened. And then at last the West Indian woman started to sob. Still not a word was spoken and after a while the visitor got up and went.

The person involved here was not ordained, and issues of touch have become increasingly difficult in our age, but that is still a vivid picture of what a priest may be called to do on behalf of an individual, a family, a school or a community. To share the pain and release the healing.

Carrying the pain

Any one of the priest's parishioners may experience some kind of unhappy fracture in their world on any day. Both they and we never know when we wake up what life-changing event may await. The world is hard-wired for life, love and the pursuit of happiness, but in a world of distortions and injustices many people experience much worse, and when the fracture opens up at someone's feet the priest is expected to be there.

I had only been in the parish a few weeks when the message came that the little granddaughter of some members of our congregation had been tragically killed when her mother's car had rolled backwards down the drive with her daughter right behind it. As I walked the short distance to the grandparents' house I felt completely devoid of words to say or prayers to offer. It was an utterly terrible event and nothing could reduce the tragedy in any degree whatsoever. All I could do was be there with them and soak up the edges of their pain. My own word-less confusion was all I had to contribute.

What the priest offers in these dark situations is a silent witness to another Presence. The presence of God is probably not openly acknowledged because the naming of any Name seems almost blasphemous on the holy ground of people's grief. However, the priest has a symbolic identity which points to the

Quiet One who bears the pain of the world. 'He has borne our griefs and carried our sorrows' (Isaiah 53.4), but he uttered no word (v. 7). By being there, not trying to make any sense of the tragedy – for there is none – the priest represents another broken life, that of Jesus, and, without saying anything, the priest is offering a source of present comfort and future hope. The priest is not a saviour but, like the Saviour he or she serves, comes with humanity, vulnerability and utter reliance on the presence and grace of God.

Priests may also have to exercise this pain-bearing role for a community. They may have to go and take an assembly or talk with staff when a popular teacher dies suddenly. With other representative figures they may have to carry the pain on behalf of a whole town when terrible murders shake the community to its core, as in Lockerbie, Dunblane, or Soham – the names themselves conjure up the massive emotions released by the appalling events that occurred there. The priest is there to help the community stay on its feet, to provide somewhere for people to take their bewilderment and pain, and to offer rituals of grief and transition. Communities are in shock and the priest stands in the middle of the shattered landscape, not above it, and models a capacity to survive and eventually to move on. But the hidden cost to the priest may be immense. Priests in this situation present themselves, their souls and bodies to be a living sacrifice, holy and acceptable to God (Romans 12.1).

I once talked to a priest who had been in a subway under one of the twin towers in New York when the hijacked plane went into it on September 11th, 2001. The story of his survival in that mayhem and the instinctive pastoral ministry both he and other priests offered in those unholy hours held me spell-bound but reminded me again of how crucial it is to have people with disciplines of prayer and compassion in situations such as that. Most priests will be faced with situations nothing like as dramatic as that but the principles of silent witness, stable presence, and pain-bearing remain true. They are no super-heroes, standing tall and strong in the midst of chaos, but, with all their own vulnerability, they represent the community of faith seeking to be available to others in the name of Christ. At funerals priests have the great but exhausting privilege of carrying people who may be in various states of emotional collapse, through a complex social, psychological and spiritual process. They have the opportunity of accompanying people through a key transition in their lives. The expectations are heavy and the stakes are high. So too is the cost. The priest may emerge from such a service emotionally exhausted.

All priests, after a time in ministry, know the experience of being overwhelmed by the pain around them. A young curate handling a vacancy was taking a funeral for a popular 40-year-old who had thrown himself in front of a train on New Year's Eve. An hour before the funeral the man's father had a heart attack and died. The priest could hardly think what to say as the mother prepared to bury her son and watched her husband's body removed from the house. The curate then had another funeral to take, then a burial of ashes, followed by a wedding interview. No wonder there are times when our margins are slender. Priests have to do their best to soak up the pain that spills all over the place, and then squeeze it out into the capacious heart of God through their prayers at night. They also need good support from people of wisdom, skill and prayerfulness – spiritual directors, colleagues, families and friends. We cannot bear these things alone.

Sometimes, of course, the priest will be the recipient of a person's anger against life, God and the universe. It may come through a tirade of abuse or a more polite bitterness, but we know when we're receiving it and it isn't a good place to be. Our best response is not to tighten up and find our own ways of getting in some sharp retaliation, but rather to return to the centre of our being, to the Lord of grace, and to operate out of that deep well of security and generosity. 'Do not be overcome by evil, but overcome evil with good' (Romans 12.21).

The ministry of reconciliation

Sometimes we are able to help others to be relieved of their pain – though 'not I, but Christ' (Galatians 2.20). This may occur especially through the ministry of reconciliation when the assurance of God's forgiveness lifts weights of all sizes from people's shoulders. The means of this ministry may be formal confession or informal (but serious) conversation. The result should be the same – a conviction that God's forgiveness is absolute and guaranteed. In this ministry of reconciliation the priest encounters all the complexity of human bewilderment and failure, mystery and passion, not only in the penitent but also sometimes in him- or herself as well. We also encounter the wide range of images of God that people enjoy or suffer. Our ministry needs to reflect back to people the life-giving God of the gospel whose love overflows constantly into his world and into our lives. We also need to encourage people not to let their mistakes cause them to retreat into living fearfully and cautiously, but to continue to live boldly and fully, with the risk of being wrong, making mistakes and falling into sin, but with the promise of abundance and the safety net of forgiveness.

In a wider sense the whole of a priest's ministry can be framed as a ministry of reconciliation. 'God . . . reconciled us to himself through Christ, and has given us the ministry of reconciliation' (2 Corinthians 5.18). We try to point to the One who holds all things together and is inexorably drawing everything towards its final integration in Christ (Ephesians 1.10). This work of reconciliation takes us from personal issues to political issues, from evangelism to social action, always with the goal of seeing the 'go-between' Spirit of God repair fractures, create harmony and establish further bridgeheads for the *shalom* of God.

Carrying pain in the congregation

'To live is to change, and to become perfect is to have changed often.' These often-quoted words of John Henry Newman

It looked like a long night at the confessional

need to carry a health warning for parish priests. To change in the local church is often to invoke fire and fury that makes the Reformation seem quite tame. Religion operates so deeply at the roots of what people believe about the world and about themselves that change can be a huge threat. That's a tribute to the importance of faith and the way we express it, but it's a major health hazard for the clergy. Very often the priest has both to manage the conflict and to internalize the pain people feel. The 'early-adopters' of a new idea are eager to move on; the solid centre are considering it; the traditionalists are getting into 'over-my-dead-body' mode. Everybody is in danger of frustration or anger, but the priest has to minister to them all.

Of course, conflicts may arise for all sorts of other reasons, good old-fashioned sin being just one of them. But however they arise, they require some form of conflict resolution. This may come from attentive pastoral care, or from trained mediators found either inside or outside the diocese. I've learned much since I supposedly dismissed the choir! When the protests erupted and the press got hold of it I was suddenly out of my depth and I had no tools to help me deal with the situation. Except one; I locked myself in church and lay in distress and prayer before the altar. Perhaps the main thing I learned was that whatever is going on in the *fracas* around us, the task of the priest is to be a stable presence, to be available, to sweep up the pain of others, and to ask people repeatedly to trust the process of conflict-resolution. Eventually one can hope that a wider vision will be found that includes and unites the conflicted parties in a win/win reconciliation. There are of course skills in the planned management of change that should be employed prior to this sad stage of breakdown and conflict-resolution. There is a formidable body of knowledge in this area now and churches can avail themselves of it.

There is a darker situation that priests sometimes have to address and that is when they come face to face with real pathology in people or communities. Even able, faithful clergy can be badly damaged by dysfunctional communities. Carrying that sort of pain for others can be dangerous and priests need to protect themselves and be protected by others, including those who have oversight of them. All priests need to be in spiritual direction and some may need psychotherapeutic help from time to time. This is a sombre note to strike but it reflects our growing understanding of how communities and congregations can occasionally operate, and it is better to be forewarned.

Intercession as bearing the pain with God and being co-creators with God

Another way of keeping vigil with a damaged world is by intercession. In the ordination service the bishop declares that priests are to 'resist evil, support the weak, defend the poor, and intercede for all in need'. The last phrase belongs with the previous three. Intercession is a way of standing in the gap and holding open to God those parts of God's world that are in need of renewal, whether those parts are individual lives or communities or nations. If we believe intercession is truly worthwhile then it's here that great issues of faith, social order and human destiny are being hammered out, or where people's health and well-being are being restored or maintained. Intercession isn't for the faint-hearted but it offers people the joy of co-creating a better world with the Lord of all Creation.

However, intercession should not simply be a lonely chore because it's not just the priest who wants to pray. Priests will want to find ways for the whole people of God to keep alive the high privilege of co-operating with God in prayer. This may involve prayer lists, prayer trees, stick-on notes, local and international maps, candles, picture boards, and many other creative methods, as well as imaginative ways of interceding in public worship. Shared intercession is a wonderful opportunity of loving service, open to people of all ages and abilities, all backgrounds and personality types.

Nevertheless, the one person who cannot escape the responsibility of intercession is the priest. It's an integral part of a calling to a particular place that the priest is to pray for the people there. 'Will you be diligent in prayer . . . ? By the help of God, I will,' goes the ordination service. Not only is prayer always used in the gracious economy of God, but also people are greatly reassured when they know the priest is praying regularly and expectantly for the parish. Sometimes that prayer may be less than exciting, but then you can say the same about many of the meals we've eaten over the years and yet we've still needed them to stay alive and well. Sometimes the prayer will be costly and painful as we bear friends, neighbours and unknown others to God. And sometimes the weight will seem overwhelming.

Pain-bearing doesn't sound like a very welcome part of the priestly task, but it is a huge service to people and communities. The pain comes in many forms in a broken world with wounded people. Priests are not made of iron; they share the brokenness with everyone else. But their special dark privilege is to be pain bearers, keeping vigil with a damaged world until God finally puts all the world to rights in his new creation.

8

Wounded companion:
Sharing the journey

The priest as pastor

A man was seriously ill in hospital. He claimed to be a non-believer. A parish priest came and sat with him and held his hand, not saying a word. After some considerable time the man said, 'You know, you lot can be very comforting at times.' The priest smiled and said nothing. Eventually the priest knew he had to move on. He took his hand away and as he did so he said, 'Now remember, even though I'm taking my hand away, God never takes his hand away.' The patient's eyes flashed. 'There you go!' he protested. 'You just can't resist it, can you?'

As we have had cause to notice in the last chapter, the priest is often most helpful when he or she is silent. It's very hard to resist the temptation to offer words of comfort or empathy, or in some way to suggest some kind of interpretative framework for a person going through a stressful experience. Nevertheless, the really important gift is accompaniment, in the manner of Christ, for whom actions were very often more important than words.

The huge privilege of the priest is to be given access to people's lives and struggles at their most vulnerable points. It's not a privilege to take for granted. Every person we meet is someone whom Jesus takes very seriously (not the same as solemnly), and therefore the priest as a pastor needs to see each encounter as completely unique, and each person's life as one that's deep in detail. Indeed, it's a useful rule-of-thumb for a priest to try and view every ministerial action as if it is the first and last time he or she has ever done it. At least that keeps our attention level high, impossible though it may eventually become to maintain that intensity.

A ministry of compassion and challenge

The roots of Christian pastoral care are found in the twin attributes of compassion and challenge. When Jesus encountered a man with leprosy we read (in Mark 1.41) that he snorted in indignation at such a distortion of God's high intention for this man. When he met two blind men in Jericho he was 'moved with compassion', and gave them their sight (Matthew 20.34). He had the same response to the widow at Nain who had tragically just lost her only son – though that didn't last long (Luke 7.11–17). You feel that same compassion in so many of the healings of Jesus. He interrupts his sermon in a synagogue when he sees a crippled woman struggling in at the back. She's horrendously bent over; her body looks so brittle you would think it would snap. Jesus is appalled at her plight and words of healing fly out of him, much to the consternation of those who like their religion properly controlled (Luke 13.10–17). Compassion is at the root of Jesus' ministry and likewise it's fundamental to the priest's pastoral task.

Yet there is a complicating factor in this positive portrayal of the pastoral role of the priest. Even a skin-deep consideration of the ministry of Jesus reveals a man whose pastoral relationships were often profoundly uncomfortable. Contact with Jesus meant change. You couldn't simply count on a hug and a handkerchief. The woman caught with her lover had to change her life-style. A young man with a lot of money had to give it all away. A blind man had to be sure he really wanted his sight, with all the loss of a beggar's privileges that went with it. In other words, Jesus' compassion had a challenging edge to it, and it's here that priestly pastoral care comes under a harsh spotlight. It's easy to be gentle; it's less easy to risk the unpopularity that goes with asking the hard questions which are sometimes necessary for a deeper transformation. When the high-flying executive lost his job, how far was his single-minded pursuit of money and status a deeper problem? When the teenager was arrested how far did his parents recognize the imprint of their own dysfunctional family life? When the leaders of the Mothers' Union got into an unseemly fight, did they see the contribution of their own long-term manipulative strategies? These are the hard questions that determine whether our pastoral care is characterized by courage as well as compassion.

The ministry of the Good Shepherd wasn't just to keep the flock safe; it was to guide them to new pasture. It was to help individuals and communities prepare for the coming of God's new Kingdom. He wasn't concerned just to patch up the old creation; he was preparing people for the new one. In Mel Gibson's remarkable and bloody film *The Passion of the Christ* there's an extraordinary moment on the Via Dolorosa when Jesus falls over yet again and Mary rushes up to him as she had done so often before when he was a child. On the ground, amid the dirt and sweat and blood, Jesus looks at his mother and says to her, 'See, mother, I make all things new.' Biblical accuracy is sacrificed to theological significance at this moment in the film, but the point is well made. Jesus always saw the future Kingdom beckoning, and the potential in everyone to display the divine imprint. So too the priest tries to balance compassion and challenge in order that the person involved in the pastoral encounter might glimpse the longer trajectories of the Kingdom of God in his or her own life.

A ministry of relationships

It may be possible for a grumpy priest to have an effective ministry but I very much doubt it. The core of a valued

Sometimes counselling seemed an uphill struggle

ministry is a network of good relationships. A priest has to establish his or her human credibility before anything else. At its most basic, in parish ministry, if people know they matter, anything is possible; if they don't think they matter, nothing will happen. A new priest can make or break his or her ministry in those first few weeks of pastoral encounters. Word gets around!

It's patently unnecessary for a new priest to establish that he's 'no pushover' or that she's 'got clear boundaries'. All that can come later. What people want to know is whether this person cares. Is he or she interested or distant, encouraging or cool, a listener or a compulsive talker? Is the priest a front-foot person or a back-foot person? Does she smile easily or frown at the first opportunity? Is he interested in other people or concerned mostly about himself and his role? People suss these things out very quickly. Above all, they sense whether the priest is kind. Kindness sounds like an impossibly flaky quality but actually it's one of the characteristics people remember most about a priest. Genuine kindness can't be manufactured to order; it's a fruit of the Spirit, growing from a life hidden in Christ.

The priest is a creator and shaper of community and, as such, relationships are of the essence. We live in a relational (rather than institutional) society and therefore the quality of our ecclesial communities is a prime focus of the priest's concern. Warm, purposeful, engaged communities are attractive. Lukewarm, argumentative, walled-in communities attract no-one. Many people have enough dysfunctionality elsewhere in their lives without needing to take on a dysfunctional church as well. As in so many other ways, the priest has a major influence on the tone and style of the church, so rule number one is to be a pastor, first and last. If priests love their communities and communities love their priests, then everything else becomes possible.

A ministry of attentiveness

You're at a social gathering and the person you're talking to is clearly not interested in the conversation. Eye contact is sporadic; he's often looking over your shoulder or watching someone else walk by. He doesn't listen to what you've said, mumbling something inappropriate in response. Eventually he spots a way out and jumps at it with unseemly enthusiasm. The whole experience has been deeply embarrassing.

On the other hand, there have been times when someone has listened to you with real care and interest. Eye contact has been close, though not threatening. Your listener has obviously attended thoroughly to what you've said; his follow-up questions have been thoughtful and astute. It's as if there has been no-one else in the room; your listener has given himself completely to you. You feel heard, known and valued.

We've all probably had both experiences and we know which one is better. The priest has the problem of being forever with people to whom he or she is supposed to be attentive, and it's tiring. But if we fail to listen carefully, people know. And if we try to put on a mask (which is inevitable at times) and it slips, the damage can be immense. Pastoral ministry can be exhausting. It also involves listening to the bass line of a conversation, not just the melody. Deep things may be afoot. The throwaway lines are the key ones that give away the anxieties. Listen; always listen. And this applies even when people don't greatly return the compliment. People often talk easily about themselves but fail to express much interest in the life and times of the priest, and that can leave us feeling somewhat hurt and devalued. We simply have to accept that. It's not intentional and it's part of the cost of being a good listener.

Not only must we attend fully and carefully, we need also to remember what we've been told. If we ring someone up with a request for a job to be done for the church, and forget that the recipient of the call has a father who has just had a serious operation and is hanging on to life by a thread, our call may not be greatly appreciated. Most priests have made this mistake at some stage. We need to write things down – and pray for a forgiving laity.

Professional detachment is a much over-valued skill in our society. Priests have professional skills too and discernment is one of them, but they also need to hold to the gift of godly attentiveness.

A limited ministry

It's important for priests to be as aware of their limitations as of their gifts in pastoral ministry. In the first place, we all have our disabilities. We are not omni-competent pastors dispensing boundless care and wisdom. We bring our own wounds to ministry and hope they won't get in the way, or even that they may be used by God in the healing of others. We need always to be opening ourselves to our own healing through the grace of God and the safe people God gives us. Pastoral ministry is unsettling. It's unsettling when I meet a saint and feel wrong-footed by that person's unpolished beauty. It's unsettling when I meet a sinner, a trusted parishioner who I previously thought was beyond reproach. It's even more unsettling when I find that the sinner is myself and yet again I've misjudged my capacity for failure. I've always found one of the wisest pieces of advice in the New Testament is in 1 Corinthians 10.12: 'If you think that you are standing, watch out that you do not fall.' We are all disabled pilgrims.

In the second place, we aren't infinite in capacity. When I was a Diocesan Youth Officer I organized a huge camping weekend for hundreds of young people, complete with mainstage concerts, 20 workshops, worship in the cathedral, midnight movies, 24-hour coffee bar and so on. Towards the end of it I was in complete collapse with physical and mental symptoms that worried me considerably. My recovery from this nervous exhaustion was steady but slow, and it taught me many things about my own limitations and the need for wisdom in stewarding my enthusiasms. It also taught me not to minimize the experience of people suffering from stress.

In the third place we need to recognize the limitations in our expertise. We mustn't try to be a counsellor on the basis of a six-week course at theological college. A wise priest knows the value of referrals and has a wide knowledge of the services available. Above all, a priest is always a learner. We have to ask daily for what the ordination collect calls 'the needful gifts of grace', to which I would add, 'the needful gift of humility'. There's no such place as the priestly promised land where all skills have been acquired and the rest is repetition. I remember the embarrassment of being in a hospital ward visiting one person when the chaplain came round, stood in the middle of the ward and sprayed trivial bonhomie around the room, avoiding engagement with anyone, confident in his own role and overbearing manner. When he left, the ward was stunned and I was all the more convinced that priestly ministry is for humble learners. The astonishing truth, of course, is that God too is humble and hands over his life to us, asking us to imitate the humility of his Son (Philippians 2.5–8).

In the fourth place pastoral care is not meant to emanate just from the priest. Indeed he or she offers very little towards the sum of human love and care generated by a local church. Priestly ministry is rooted in the ministry of all the baptized and the people of God are always at work in the close fabric of any community, offering practical care, a listening ear over a cup of tea, and often heroic feats of self-sacrifice. Priestly humility is essential before the extraordinary level of compassion that characterizes most Christian congregations. Nevertheless priests also have a ministry to this network of care and will seek to harness all this natural compassion by setting up some form of pastoral visiting team to care for the long-term sick, the bereaved, the housebound and others. He or she may set up a healing team to pray (responsibly) with those who want it or to organize healing services or a 'prayer chain' to activate supportive prayer at short notice. The combined pastoral resources of the local church should be a huge encouragement to hard-pressed priests as they minister in the company of the whole people of God.

Lastly, priests are limited by the very nature of pastoral care as open-ended and messy. We have to resist the desire to sort things out and close the file. People aren't like that. We all live with perennial issues, ambiguities, questions, and problematic characteristics. Pastoral care is bound to be an exercise in loose ends as we accompany people for a time and then step aside as they carry on the journey which is rightly their own.

A ministry of accompaniment and prayer

'More tea, vicar?' is a line that will never entirely disappear from British culture. Nevertheless, having a drink with people is a crucial part of pastoral ministry, although I would broaden the category of beverage! What matters is the quality of conversation. It's good for the priest to know quite clearly what the purpose of a conversation really is. It may simply be to let someone know he or she matters and is remembered, but it may be much more. It may be to introduce the church to newcomers or to nurture the faith of a baptism couple. It may be to offer space to someone with a serious decision to make or someone who you sense is losing their way. It may be to ask the question, 'Well, how are you and God then?' and see where it leads. It may be to stir up a possible vocation to some form of ministry. But time for visiting is too rare a commodity these days for a general tea-drinking ministry. Visiting usually has to be prioritized on the Church Council (early on), the ill, troubled and bereaved, newcomers (very important), and key leaders. Jesus spent most of his ministry working closely with his key leaders; he knew what he was doing.

On a placement during my ordination training I can remember being affronted by a priest who declared he did most of his visiting by telephone. I now understand what he meant. Time is limited but pastoral contact is essential. There are many times when a phone call or a little note is all that is needed, although the point is of course to get on and do it, rather than just to think about doing it.

All the priest's pastoral ministry needs to be prayerful. Prayer as we go to a visit; prayer offered at the end of a visit, prayer as we leave a visit laden with much trust, prayer as the days go on, prayer when the phone is put down, prayer when the note is written. The One we want to make present for people is Christ, in whatever way is most needed. Pastoral praying ensures that this ministry has depth and quality because it's centred on God and his grace, not on us and our charm.

One final point: most pastoral ministry is invisible and should remain so. If the priest starts to ask who is noticing his or her sacrificial ministry, a line has been crossed. Similarly if the priest judges the value of a visit to a person in need by whether they might start coming to church or not, a dangerous borderland has been reached. Each life has infinite value in its own right; none is a means to some other end.

The essence of pastoral ministry is that Christ in the priest meets Christ in the other person. The rest is detail.

9

Weather-beaten witness:
Discerning the Kingdom

The priest as apostle

One bishop I know aims to spend half his working life outside
the church. He's trying to be properly apostolic, as his role
requires. The apostle is one who knows that he is 'sent' in the
way the first apostles were sent to bear witness to the crucified
and risen Lord. He or she is sent with a message of liberating
love to the ends of the earth. The priest is called out of
'Jerusalem' (the known territory of the Church), into Samaria
(the slightly less congenial settings) and thence to the ends of
the earth (the scary places – Acts 1.8).

RⁿN

After his induction, Gerald met the leaders of other denominations

For some years I have been deeply involved in a bid to have the twin-site monastery of Wearmouth / Jarrow designated by the World Heritage Committee of UNESCO as a World Heritage Site. This has been based on the enormous significance to Western culture of the Venerable Bede, one of history's true intellectual giants, and the impact this remote monastic community in the north-east of England had on the rest of Europe. Chairing this bid has involved a very large expenditure of time as our steering group, management group, working groups, consultants, project officers and others have busied themselves on the task. There have been large sums of money to raise, politicians to lobby, and the press to mobilize. Partnerships have been formed with the local authorities, English Heritage, the regional development agency, universities, churches, the Port of Tyne, the National Glass Centre, library and museum services and many more.

Why? Why has so much effort been worthwhile? Simply because it puts the Church and the Christian faith at the heart of a venture that could lead to major benefits for the local community. It's a Kingdom project. It could bring major developments in tourism, education and the economy, as well as enhancing the confidence, profile and self-image of two fairly deprived parts of the north-east of England. And it's all based on a monk and a monastery. If the Kingdom of God is a healed creation (Hans Küng) then this is part of that healing.

The Church has an unfortunate tendency to consume its members. Christians are drawn deeper and deeper into church-related activities, forgetting that the energy of the Holy Spirit is centrifugal, constantly trying to throw us out into the community beyond the Church. The reason why so much church life fails to inspire people may be that the range of its vision is too small. Our task is to work with the God of creation and redemption to re-shape the world to be ready for the time when all things will be gathered up in Christ (Ephesians 1.10). The vision is enormously exciting. It isn't about gathering small groups of Christians into safe places. It's about renewing the face of the earth.

The priest as 'Kingdom-spotter'

The image I've chosen for this apostolic role is that of a weather-beaten witness. When we step outside the comparative safety of the church's life (assuming hand-to-hand fighting hasn't broken out at the last PCC meeting) we find the weather is distinctly unpredictable. In some parts of our post-Christendom society the presence of the Church is welcomed and affirmed; in others it's misunderstood and marginalized. It's hard to know whether we're going to need a summer shirt or wet-weather gear.

The priest is a public, representative figure. This is unavoidable. No longer can the priest hide in the anonymity of the pews, as in pre-ordination days. We are on the line; we can't be on the fence. What we say and do matters because it will be interpreted as being the words and actions of the wider Church. People judge the Church by how its chief representatives behave. They may even judge God by the same measure. It's an alarming responsibility, but one redolent with possibility. If the priest 'gets it right' in a meeting with the local authority, with education chiefs, with regional development officers, with police chiefs or leaders of business, then the consequential benefits can be immense. A context of respect and trust is created; partnerships are formed which might become friendships. We live in a relational society and relationships can be productive for the Kingdom or not. The local priest may be the best (or worst) advert the Church has got.

The deep and threatening question the priest has to ask is whether he or she is committed first of all to the Church or the Kingdom. The temptation is to serve the piper who calls the tune (pays the money), but the real questions are: who is the Piper and what's the real tune? Of course Church and Kingdom shouldn't need to compete for the priest's attention. The Church is the sacrament of the Kingdom and the contours of the Church's life should reflect the shape of the coming Kingdom, the Kingdom on which Jesus 'cut the ribbon', announcing its arrival in himself and his own ministry. Nevertheless, institutions being what they are, we sometimes do have to make a choice between Church and Kingdom because the Church can easily become self-serving and consume all our energy. The apostle is sent to the world because God loved that world so much that he sent his only Son to it (John 3.16). It's not for us to change the rules.

The priest's task is often to be a 'Kingdom-spotter'. What is God doing out there, and how can the church join in? Wherever there are issues of justice and peace, we can be sure God is involved. Wherever the environment and the 'integrity of creation' are at stake, we can guarantee God's commitment. Wherever the poor are struggling to find a voice we can pretty much take it for granted that God is on their side. The important thing is to make sure that we aren't hijacked by the need to write the vicar's letter for the magazine or prepare the PCC agenda – unless, of course, it's to put those very issues on it. Priests will try to make sure that the biggest issues and priorities take the first slice of their time. They'll review their priorities, probably with a colleague in the context of ministerial review. They'll undoubtedly try to 'make the main thing the main thing'. But they know the *urgent* will constantly threaten the *important*.

Ownership and partnership

The other temptation is to try and 'own' the Kingdom-activities that we spot – or otherwise not to be interested in them. Christians love to baptize a social project and take it into the family of church activities. And if that isn't possible then we 'let them get on with it'. The test has to be not whether a project gives glory to the church but whether it gives benefit to the community. If a project is good, it's good! It doesn't need to be baptized. Nevertheless, there are some social projects that will come about because the local church discerns the need and takes the initiative. In the area I know best I think of an Action Station community project that houses an advice centre, credit union and café. I think of a Food Stop in a town centre, several family centres, and work with asylum seekers. I see the burgeoning of wraparound childcare facilities and lunch clubs for the elderly. I delight in the arrival of a community arts chaplain and all the new youth ministers springing up to work in schools, churches and neighbourhoods. All this is a sign that the churches of God recognize the call to serve their localities, and if necessary to pioneer the work, to own it and persist with it.

Better still, however, if the local church can be in partnership with others. Partnership is always better than flying solo. The priest is often the person who goes and finds partners for 'Kingdom-projects'. Those partners will sometimes be surprised to have an approach from the church, perhaps even nonplussed, but soon enough they are likely to be delighted, particularly when we tell them what we bring to the table. Many local officials – be they politicians, planners, educationalists, regeneration boards, local strategic partnerships or others – are unaware of how rich the resources of the local churches are. In one small borough they could hardly believe it when the churches demonstrated through an excellent, professional report that they represented 81 faith-based organizations, with 443 group activities a week and 14,000 users of their facilities. The priest doesn't go to the table a pauper.

Much of the New Testament revolves around the conflict between the status quo of the Roman Empire and the new world of the Kingdom. By being at the forefront of the renewal of our neighbourhoods, priests are bearing witness to the central theological conviction that 'Jesus is Lord, and Caesar is not' (N. T. Wright). The priest's apostolic role is to be faithful to the witness of the apostles who demonstrated that the risen, ascended Lord is concerned for the flourishing of the whole human person. Presenting Jesus as the One who calls us to walk with him has to imply a concern for the conditions in which that walk takes place, with all its variables of wealth, education, health and opportunity. By all means we must present the converting Christ, but we also need to present the compassionate Christ, the one who wants every part of us to be saved and healed. And, wonderfully, when we plant the flag of the Kingdom by challenging injustice and poverty, it sometimes also leads to an opportunity to plant the flag by bearing witness to the Lord we serve – the whole Christ for the whole person. I think of a tough northern mayor who had long ago rejected faith but was intrigued by the sheer attractive quality of the local priest's life and commitments. He was ready to talk.

Apostles together: the power of genuine collaboration

There are two vital dimensions of this book that are sometimes visible and sometimes not. One is the dimension of collaboration with lay people; the other is collaboration with ecumenical partners.

The whole people of God have an apostolic identity, and it's much more effective than that of the priest working alone. A visitor to a clergy meeting asked them where their churches were. One said his was on the main street, just by the library. Another said his was on the road to the station. A third said: 'Where's my church? Right now they're spread out all over town.' The potential witness of baptized Christians in a given locality is enormous. Here are people active in every sector of society, in banks and offices and schools, in clubs and leisure centres and darts teams, in families and friendships and every voluntary organization imaginable. The task of the priest is to equip God's people for joyful, confident witness to the hope that is in them. For that confident witness to become widespread there needs to be a kind of 'climate change' in the life of the Church, but there's no greater prize. Support for this lay witness, of course, comes from the sector ministers and ministers in secular employment (MSEs) who exercise this ministry day by day. Most people between the ages of 20 and 55 spend most of their significant time at work. This is where the gospel has to be embodied and explored and our sector ministers and MSEs need every encouragement.

The other crucial dimension of our apostolicity is our collaboration with ecumenical partners. We have a plethora of ecumenical instruments, Local Ecumenical Partnerships, covenants and other enabling legislation to encourage us 'to be one, that the world may believe' (John 17.21). These structures are very important, even if Jesus might wonder if that's what he'd really meant. However, the plain truth is that ecumenism usually depends on good, trusting, personal relationships. When seven church leaders from the north-east went to Rome together for a short pilgrimage, the ground gained was worth five years of ecumenical meetings. Time spent on the things that matter to us, our deep experiences of faith and doubt, and our hopes for the gospel in our time – all this is tremendously important, and leads to the deep and joyful realization that, for all of us, Christ is our life, and in him we are already one. This means that friendship, prayer and eating together are the life-blood of worthwhile ecumenism. And when we discover the points at which we depart from each other we need to go *through* the barrier of disappointment and not use it as an excuse to retreat to base. Strangeness can be a doorway to discovery.

The deeper reality is that in the Western Church we can no longer enjoy the luxury of parallel church traditions. The urgency of the task of mission in a post-Christendom culture and the decline in conventional church-going is leading us to a humble acceptance of the prayer of Christ that we should all be one. We can do no other. We have to start from the premise of baptismal unity. We've gone past the stages of competition and co-existence, and even that of co-operation. We've arrived at the stage of commitment and need to aim for the goal of full communion. We must leave behind any notion of checking up on each other to see whether 'they' make the grade. Instead we need to respond to the divine invitation as Peter did when he looked into the faces of Cornelius and his Gentile friends and realized: 'God gave them no less a gift than he gave us when we put our trust in the Lord Jesus Christ' (Acts 11.17). That's a sure and gracious ground on which to build our unity. The time has come when we need to gather together the Christians of all denominations in a particular locality and say to them: 'You are the singular Body of Christ in this place; how then might you live his life together?'

The weather-beaten witness

When you meet people who have earned their living off the land you realize how deeply marked they are by the experience. The wind-blown features, the tanned leather skin, the far-seeing eyes, all tell the story. So too the weather-beaten witness to the Kingdom of God who has spent much time beyond the centrally heated security of the Church. There's a wisdom, a knowingness about such a person. To a greater or lesser extent all God's priests need to gain some of that quality of weather-beaten wisdom.

The Kingdom of God which a priest is committed to discerning, welcoming and nurturing is the arena where God's will is obeyed and cherished. It's among us now, through the acts of God in the life of Jesus, and it's yet to come through the denouement we call the Parousia. Hidden, mysterious, unexpected, essentially simple – it's on its way.

10

Iconic presence:
Identifying with the community

The priest as parson

The word 'parson' seems to come from another age, one of crinolines and cucumber sandwiches. It speaks of a time of deference and respect for established social hierarchies, in which the parson occupied a middling position. It could create interesting expectations.

A vicar was called to see a man who was very ill. The man's wife took the vicar upstairs and they found the sick man with his eyes closed. The vicar took his wrist and felt for the pulse. 'I'm afraid he's gone,' he said to the wife solemnly. 'No I ain't,' said the man indignantly. 'Hush, dear,' said his wife, 'parson knows best.'

Even without that level of deference there remains a cultural nostalgia for the bicycling parson who visited every afternoon, knew all the village children by name and, though somewhat eccentric, was always there at the heart of the community, and always had time. For understandable reasons this stereotype has become attached to George Herbert whose short ministry near Salisbury was immortalized in his book *The Country Parson*. Better that than the other stereotype – the bumbling television parson, naive and ineffective.

This image of the country parson is tied up with a view of the church that has all but passed away. This view identified the church as 'a building, a vicar and the Sunday services', and it drew on the centuries-old territorial assumptions of the Church of England. Now of course the territorial assumptions have changed markedly. People have multiple existences, based on work, friendship groups, leisure activities and shopping habits, and where people live is of considerably less significance to them. A third of Britons don't even know their neighbours, let alone the vicar. This seismic shift in people's perceptions of where they belong has meant that the Church is having to re-think its mission strategy to incorporate networks, flexibility, provisionality and diversity, in order to express what it means to be a Christian in the company of others (that is, the Church). These are exciting times.

Nevertheless, particular people and special places will always be vital to the Church's life. Christianity is an embodied, incarnational faith; people matter. It's also a faith associated with particular places and the events associated with them. The tradition of special 'thin' places of pilgrimage, where God has shone through the mist, is an authentic mark of a faith connected to holy land, not only to a new heaven but also to a new earth. Earth, sacred earth, is the *adamah* from which *adam* was formed (Genesis 2). Both people and place matter to this robust, earthy faith (although they cannot constrict a faith that also has a tradition of wandering, journeying, no abiding city, 'no place to rest his head').

The priest as icon and sacrament

It's important that the priest doesn't let these images of icon and sacrament go to his or her head! Nevertheless priests cannot avoid people identifying them with the being and life of the church. The dog-collar gives it away. The growing habit of clergy not to wear this immediate signifier may be understandable as an attempt to identify with so-called 'ordinary people' (who are they?), but it can leave some people feeling deceived, and it can also deprive us of some excellent opportunities for contact. A self-supporting minister I know works in a big supermarket and the occasional but regular wearing of his clerical collar opens up all sorts of pastoral and 'apologetic' conversations.

Moreover, why should the priest be ashamed of representing Christ and his community? Paul, after all, gloried in his identification with Christ (Galatians 6.14). The priest has the privilege of being a kind of walking sacrament (Austin Farrer), an outward and visible sign of an inward and spiritual grace – in this case the presence of Christ in the community. Of course it puts the priest on his or her mettle. There's nowhere to hide when you get annoyed at the shop assistant's incompetence, park your car illegally ('just for a moment'), or fall asleep in the school concert. But you are also the acceptable face of the Church, the bearer of an important symbolic identity, and witness to an alternative set of meanings. The priest's presence can pose unsettling questions, previously kept locked up in the basement of people's consciousness. Even more significantly, the priest can make Christ present for people and gives them permission to believe and to pray.

This iconic role is as much exercised by the leader of a church plant, an after-school congregation or a faith-based community project as by the vicar of a country parish. Whether wearing recognizable symbols or not, the leader will be identified with the project. People need to know who the focal person is and where leadership and stability is to be found. Fresh expressions of emerging church often focus on someone with a charismatic personality. This is an advantage in terms of public profile and gifts of leadership, but it's a problem when the project needs to move on to its second phase and the leadership changes. This is why a leadership team should always be established to multiply the gifts and dilute the dependency.

A college chaplain I knew used to speak of trying to perfect 'the art of strategic presence'. He needed to be visible at the right places at the right times, and he could then allow himself to get on with other things, or be with his family, at other times. That's one of the arts of the priest as an iconic presence in a community, be it a parish, a school, a hospital, a workplace or a new form of church. If the priest can be seen, he or she can be used. It's the incarnational principle of ministry. Just being there allows God to make the connections. Two women priests I know have wonderful ministries in their local pubs. From there they organize funerals, offer counsel, hear confessions, bless pendants, and talk about God. Not every priest can get away with it, but if you can, do!

Thus the priest as parson (God's 'person') is able to develop the art not only of strategic presence but also of strategic action. He or she will come to know when to take an initiative in celebration or mourning, when to put energy into a particular community need, and when to offer a ritual to carry people's significant transitions. Handling these moments sensitively and well creates a huge penumbra of goodwill around the church, and a great opportunity to build longer-lasting relationships. As most priests recognize, the occasional offices are similarly our best friends in mission. They give unprecedented contact with people who would never otherwise be in church, and we don't even have to go out to find the contacts – people come to us! If the priest handles the situation well, doors will then be half-open all over the community. 'Parson' may not always know best, but at least he's known to be a worthy representative of his Lord.

The importance of place

Priests share their iconic identity with the buildings that speak of faith. The churches of our diverse landscape carry the memories and half-awakened longings of many communities. The broadcaster Jeremy Paxman said:

The thing in the font had claimed another victim . . .

Church spires are the great punctuation points of the English countryside. But the religious buildings of this country not only tell where we are geographically, they tell us where we've come from. They're often the only place in a community which has a living, visible connection to the past. They hot-wire us into our history.

I once had the privilege of looking after a church with Saxon origins. It traced our path through history and was deeply loved. Similarly, when I served Canterbury Cathedral as a member of the Chapter, I was aware of its immense capacity to inspire, to challenge and to heal. The writer A. N. Wilson said:

> Not only are our parish churches and cathedrals an aesthetic feast spread out across the land, they are also a subversive challenge to our contemporary viewpoint. They are embodiments in stone, wood and glass, of our ancestors and their way of viewing the world. A few minutes in an empty church can often make our way of viewing things seem foolish or trivial compared with theirs.

The priest must therefore beware of underestimating the power of buildings. They may be cumbersome, expensive, and resistant to modern needs. There may well be too many of them and they may be in the wrong places. Nevertheless they carry a community's story and the personal stories of countless neighbours. And when they are left open during the week (pray God for courage), they are usually visited by many more people than come to worship on Sundays. These 'thin' places open a crack in people's lives through which the light of God may begin to seep. Some gentle aids to reflection can encourage the process. For example, there can be a number of prayer spaces around the church with a picture or object to focus on and the chance to respond by lighting a candle, writing a prayer request or placing a small stone on a cairn. Explanatory notices with encouragement to think or pray can be placed around the church. Prayer cards and Bible verses can be left around for visitors to take away and use at home. The careful use of lighting and imaginative decoration (not just banners and flowers – a designer would have plenty of ideas) can also enhance the visitor experience. In more popular churches, quiet recorded music can help reflective engagement with the building. A prayer walk in the churchyard can be devised using both the natural world and interesting inscriptions on gravestones, with prayers and verses of scripture on explanatory leaflets left in the church porch. These wonderful buildings can do much of our work for us.

Of the Church of England's 16,000 churches, 13,000 are listed buildings. English Heritage estimate that it would take nearly £1000 million over five years to repair all of England's listed places of worship. Congregations raise over one third of the annual sum needed – such is the affection people have for their churches. It's hard to forecast what the future holds for these inspiring buildings. Many will diversify their use, being adapted for much more than a few hours of worship a week. One church even hosts a post office. Others will have to be mothballed because they're no longer in the right place or supported by enough people. Perhaps some will emerge as contemporary 'minster' churches – resource churches for outlying fellowships that may or may not gather in existing church buildings. The shape of our usage of church buildings may change, but the need for sacred spaces will continue and probably intensify. In the absence of a worshipping culture, people's spiritual longings still search for a home. The Church has lots of homes to offer.

The old paradigm and the new

It's clear that a move is taking place in the way the Church understands its local identity. The local church is not 'a building, a vicar and the Sunday services'. The church is a community of people in mission. Nevertheless, there is a special place within the culture of that community for the priest and the building with which he or she is associated. The sacramental principle is that particular people and special places very often act as the outward signs and expressions of deeper spiritual realities. There are analogies in all areas of life. Nations need their monarchs and presidents, their flags and national anthems. Football supporters need their heroes, their uniforms and their songs. The priest need not be embarrassed at the role of parson or dismissive of the importance of church buildings. In the mercy of God human beings have been made to respond to such iconic identities. What God has joined together, let none of us put asunder.

11

Friendly irritant:
Challenging the structures

The priest as prophet

There's a well-known, and probably apocryphal, story of a theological student who took an old Bible and a pair of scissors, and carefully cut out of the Bible every reference to God's care for the poor and his demand for justice for the oppressed. It took him a long time but when he had finished the Bible literally fell apart. It was a Bible full of holes.

Priests are called to a prophetic role in the community. The Ordinal says, 'They are to resist evil, support the weak, defend the poor, and intercede for all in need.' Only so can they demonstrate that God is committed to people's holistic well-being. There is a danger, renewed in every generation, of the Church becoming so absorbed in its own internal redecoration that it forgets the majesty of its calling to be an agent of universal transformation. Paul insists that the whole of creation is waiting for the children of God to come into their own, and claim their inheritance of freedom and joy (Romans 8.19). This isn't a pocket-sized gospel.

When this holistic style of mission is exemplified by the local church something very powerful is released. In the historic Holy Trinity Church on Clapham Common you can see an old and very well-worn table. It's the table on which William Wilberforce wrote the draft of the Act to abolish slavery in that remarkable period of social reform inspired by a group of Christian lay people in the early nineteenth century. And that's the table on which the eucharist is celebrated every Sunday, thus demonstrating in the most powerful symbolic way the cohesion and holistic nature of Christian mission.

The fact that the Clapham Sect was chiefly a group of lay people is a strong endorsement of the prophetic character of the whole people of God. Nevertheless, it's often the priest who has to remind the church of its prophetic identity. The default mode for many churches is often fairly quiescent because, for many, life is exhausting enough anyway and they value the church as a place of recovery rather than a spring-board for yet more activity. However, authentic Christian living, either individually or as a community, reaches out for more, because Christianity is a social religion, and it has a sting. Jesus was a teacher and a healer but his message had a revolution-ary thrust. If he had simply taught about the way to achieve serenity he would hardly have been worth crucifying. As it is, he taught about the way to a new world and a new ordering of society, and was therefore very much worth crucifying.

Three levels of engagement

Every church is committed to doing good; that's not in dispute. What we are thinking about here is digging a bit deeper into the geology of the gospel in the community. The priest is likely to be drawn into at least three levels of community engagement. The first is *presence*. He or she often has to turn up and, in so doing, 'bless' many events, from school fund-raising concerts to meetings of the borough council. Such 'being there' shouldn't be despised. It demonstrates a shared commitment to the community's well-being, and it forms the bedrock of mutual respect and understanding from which other opportunities may flow. And after all, as Woody Allen said, 'Eighty per cent of life is just turning up'.

The next level of engagement for a priest is likely to be that of *partnership*, mentioned earlier in Chapter 9. Building on the benefits gained by being present in community life, the priest is then able to either initiate or respond to opportunities for joint action – for example, to establish an elderly people's lunch club, a detached youth work project, a community drop-in centre, a job-seekers' club or action for homeless people. Sometimes these partnerships are financially very rewarding since other partners who are well positioned to attract funding need to be able to demonstrate community involvement, and the church is clearly well networked into the community. As a result, halls may be rebuilt or refurbished, family workers appointed, projects established – and God is glorified as the slow work of new creation goes on.

The 'sting' of the gospel, however, may upset this happy equilibrium at the next level of engagement. This is the level of *prophecy*. This is where the priest may be called on by the gospel to take a stand against a clear injustice or an ethically dubious action. This is the 'tipping point' when partnership tips over into challenge and relationships may potentially sour. It's the distinction made by Dom Helder Camara, the former Bishop of Recife, when he said, 'When I give food to the poor they call me a saint. When I ask why the poor have no food they call me a Communist.' For the priest, it's an anxious moment. Good relationships, built up over a period of time, are about to be put under strain. Many in the congregation may disagree with him. The press will smell controversy and soon come calling. The bishop may get to hear of it and ring up for a friendly chat.

Theologically, the priest is having to make the distinction between discerning God's presence in blessing or in judgement. On the face of it, there may seem to be a fine line between these two, but the consequences of each are highly divergent. False prophets may be saying 'peace, peace, when there is no peace' (Jeremiah 6.14). The prophetic task is to look into the depth of events and discern their direction, either towards God's Kingdom or subtly deviating from it. Some prophetic causes are clear. When three billion people in the world live on less than two dollars a day, something needs to be said and done. When for every £1 the West gives in aid to African countries £3 comes back in debt repayment, it's obvious that the Church's campaign to cancel the debt burden of the world's poorest countries has been well founded. Similarly, climate change is now so urgent an issue it's beyond dispute that the churches should be in the front rank of pressure and protest – and putting their own houses in order.

On the other hand, some issues are less clear cut, more open to debate, or more insidiously embedded in the collective psyche, and the issue is correspondingly more complex. You can then appreciate why there don't seem to be many instances in the Bible of a prophet who applied for the job (perhaps only Isaiah, who responded to God's question, 'Who shall I send?'). It takes courage to question the arms industry when a local community is dependent on an armaments factory. It's not easy to put down a marker against corporate greed when you have a number of city financiers in the congregation. It requires great care in repudiating a bill to legalize assisted suicide when you're trying to accompany some ill people and their carers who believe it's the only humane course to take. It takes courage and pastoral wisdom to criticize Britain's military involvement in a contentious Middle Eastern crisis when you minister in an army town and many families have sons and daughters at risk. Nevertheless, the priest is an ambassador of an ethical Kingdom and cannot avoid the risks of unpopularity. The Good News of the Kingdom sometimes requires that we first point out the *bad news* of our current way of doing things.

At the same time, priests have to exercise this prophetic ministry in a way that is congruent with other aspects of their role as, for example, preachers and teachers of the inclusive love of God. Angry denunciations are usually counter-productive.

Judgementalism is distinctly unattractive. We look to the examples of men like Martin Luther King, Desmond Tutu and Dietrich Bonhoeffer for guidance on how to be both passionate and gracious, and we try to make sure we are not abusing our office, our pulpits or our status in the community.

What's at stake

Essentially the priest has a calling to help the church resist its centripetal tendency to expend its energy on its own domestic agendas. The gospel Jesus left us was not about collecting Christians into safe places but rather about transforming lives and communities until the earth is filled with the glory of God. Christians are to be the first-fruits of a new creation, the advance guard of a new humanity. The Church is to be a 'trial-run' of the Kingdom of God, where the values and habits of the Kingdom are tested before they're let loose on the world. The Church is a liberated zone, open to the Lordship of Christ, for the sake of the world.

All of this might surprise the average church-goer. It sounds remarkably high-flown and all very well for bishops and theologians to write about in their studies, but 'off the map' in terms of your average congregation trying to eke out an honest living. However, if this is the case, the task of the priest is to re-draw the map, to enlarge it and to excite people with the vision of Jesus Christ at the heart and hub of all human life. This is a challenge to our own theology as well. Perhaps we too have domesticated God into the Church's possession, our own deity, who we occasionally share with the world on a good day with a following wind. The God of Scripture will have none of this. Either God is the centre and source of all life, or he's still an idol, the God before God before God. We may say we worship the one true God while actually our commitment is to a God who thinks like us, votes like us, condemns the people we condemn, and doesn't ask any awkward questions about how we spend our money, our time and our compassion. God shares his centrality with no-one, because he shares his love with everyone. There is no inch of this earth, and no activity of humankind, of which Jesus Christ does not say, 'This is mine.'

It's this vision of God, and God's place in the Church and the world, that's at stake in our prophetic ministry. The question is not, 'Why should Christians be involved in the issues of public life?' but rather, 'On what grounds could Christians possibly withdraw from the rule of Christ in the public square?' As with every aspect of ministry, this prophetic witness is shared by the whole people of God, and lay people are often strategically positioned by their employment and commitments to be able to raise the prophetic flag. The priest, however, acts as a focus and encouragement for this ministry, and, as for lay people, this often involves being painfully exposed, misunderstood and maligned. There's almost no recourse when the press misrepresents you; you just have to ignore it, speak the truth and be consistent. Nevertheless, being prepared to step up and speak for the gospel is a matter of priestly integrity and courage.

Counting the cost

People don't often have problems with a priest – and the church that he or she serves – being committed to social action for the welfare of the community. It's very impressive to find in a recent survey that 97 per cent of Episcopal churches in the United States participate in a soup kitchen or food programme. All the churches in one town in North Carolina have a weekend called 'Operation Inasmuch' based on the promise in Matthew 25 where Jesus says, 'Inasmuch as you did it to one of the least of these my brothers and sisters, you did it to me.' These churches spend a weekend in which hundreds of Christians offer practical help to their community neighbours – they garden and clean, they clear gutters and wash cars, they provide food parcels and clothing, they mend fences and empty lofts, they look after children and take teenagers to camp. It's a huge effort – and many British churches have a similar, if less ambitious, commitment.

No-one has a problem with this. What raises the temperature is when the people of God and their priests start 'getting involved with politics'. That's how prophetic engagement is often seen, and how the media love to report it. The priest simply has to realize that he or she is entering dangerous territory. As a young priest I can remember a senior canon walking out of a eucharist at which I was presiding in protest at my praying for the Foreign Secretary who happened to be of the wrong political persuasion for my esteemed colleague. However, the priest must resist forcibly the popular claim that 'the Church shouldn't get involved with politics'. For all the previous reasons it's impossible for the Church and its priests not to be concerned about the total well-being of the community. People live in homes, have jobs, send their children to school, drive to work, go to shops and so on – which means that housing, employment, education, transport, and commerce are all automatically concerns for the Church. People don't live in religious bubbles. As Archbishop Desmond Tutu said, 'I'm puzzled as to what Bible people are reading when they say that religion and politics don't mix.' The Bible is a record of God's involvement with the whole of life, through people and politics, war and peace, kings and prophets. Jesus himself was killed at least in part because he was a powerful prophet challenging the political and religious compromises at the heart of the nation's life and destiny.

So the priest is bound to affirm that Christianity and politics do indeed mix, inevitably and sometimes dangerously, as we have seen for example in South Africa, Pakistan, Sudan, Indonesia, Central America, the old Soviet bloc countries and many more. But the priest is also bound to affirm that in the first instance he or she is concerned about political principles and not political parties. Some listeners will always jump from the one to the other as they try to label us for their convenience, but that must remain their problem and not ours. Our issue is to remain true to the gospel and not be swayed by our prejudices and obsessions. Especially beware the latter. The congregations of this land are very patient but they don't need to be harangued week after week about the price of animal feed in Turkistan or whatever our particular obsession happens to be.

The priest's best guarantee of keeping a balanced prophetic ministry comes from the life of prayer and critical engagement with the scriptures. Prophecy should never be separated from prayer. The struggle to envisage and work for a new world should never be separated from the deep resources of contemplation. In silent prayer we're faced with our own demons as well as those of the world, and God in his mercy will work on both, to defuse their power and re-instate his just and gentle rule. Regular exposure to God is our best hope of seeing beyond our own needs and fantasies and holding on to a truthful reading of the world. As ever, without a deep and growing relationship with God we're in the mist and sinking, but, with that relationship, we're safely in the hands of the living God of justice and compassion. In prayer we drive our foundations down into God, in whose presence there is no room for fantasy, vanity or error. And through the boreholes driven by our prayer, the passion of God for his world may erupt vigorously and effectively into our church and into our priestly ministry.

Part Three

THE RENEWAL OF THE CHURCH

———◆———

Gracious God,
help your Church not to dwell on the mistakes of the past,
holding us to the pain of Golgotha
and keeping us from meeting you afresh in Galilee.
Let us share instead in the renewal of your Church,
sent and strengthened by your power and love,
that we may go forever and wherever in your company
and delight in your new day,
through Jesus Christ our Lord.
Amen.

12

Creative leader:
Scanning the horizon

The priest as team leader

With a few moments' thought we can probably all bring to mind someone who was for us a truly effective leader and had a significant effect on our lives. With a little more thought we might be able to identify the characteristics that made that person so inspiring. What's more difficult is making any generalizations about those characteristics, without falling into the well-known wisdom that the secret of leadership is to find out which way people are going and then go and walk in front of them!

I think of a priest who was vicar of a large church and yet never appeared to be in a hurry. He seemed to spend a lot of time thinking and praying, and he always had time for individual conversations. He was remarkably up-to-date in what was going on in contemporary culture and seemed to have read key books and articles of both theological and social commentary. He would often advise me where to look on the internet for useful information. He knew his colleagues in leadership in the church and spent time with them; he trusted them and they responded. And, lo and behold, his church was growing.

There's a good deal of suspicion about excessive management in the Church today and we will return to that issue in Chapter 15. But at whatever level one thinks about the Body of Christ it remains also an organization of many people and any organization needs both management and leadership. It can be valuable to note the different emphases each has. Essentially (and simplistically) managers make sure things happen and leaders implement new things; managers focus on making the systems effective, leaders focus on encouraging the people who work in those systems; managers have to trouble-shoot, leaders have to look at far-reaching improvements; managers have to watch the bottom line, leaders have to watch the horizon. No organization, not even the holy society that is the Church, can flourish without being both well led and well run. Clergy have to exercise both roles but this chapter is about leadership; and I'm not talking here of respectable ordained executives, but of godly, visionary leaders, shaped by the life and leadership of Jesus.

Leaders scan the horizon

No-one can accuse Jesus of not embracing the big picture. He lived in constant awareness of Israel's story and God's action in the arena of world history. His mental and spiritual backdrop was always the call and arrival of the Kingdom of God. He saw his task within the huge narrative of God's love for the world, and he always had his eye on the future when God would gather all things to himself.

One of the clearest demands of clergy leadership is that priests never lose sight of the big picture. A thousand distractions will intervene but once a priest loses his or her holy fascination with what God is doing throughout history and throughout the world, all that remains to the priest is the detail of ecclesiastical machinery. A priest is unashamedly a leader in mission and he or she must therefore survey the context of that mission, the way the culture operates, the trends in social and political life, the intellectual movements of the times, the values and frameworks with which people survive, the books people read, the television they watch, and so on. The priest as leader has to be a cultural analyst, asking always for the wisdom and mind of Christ.

There has always seemed to me much wisdom in the old advice: 'Sometimes I sits and thinks, and sometimes I just sits.' We need space to consider and weigh the information that surrounds and threatens to overwhelm us, and to ponder the movement of the Spirit in our own lives. The Venerable Bede wrote of King Edwin that he was 'by nature a wise and prudent man, and often sat alone in silence for long periods, turning over in his mind what he should do'. Clergy leaders also need spaciousness so that the truly important is not sacrificed to the merely urgent. Activism is a snare and a delusion. We need time to think, reflect and pray.

I realize that this sounds like a counsel of perfection; I can hear my wife's hollow laughter even as I write, but the important principle is never to give up the struggle to maintain the big picture, to scan the horizon, and to understand the movements both of the spirit of the age and of the Spirit of God. To that extent a clergy leader is a liminal figure, living in the borderland between the Church and the world, the present and the future, inherited church and emerging church. Sometimes that's a lonely or an alarming place to be but, because we believe in a God who comes to us fresh from the future, more often than not we can be bearers of hope, seeing a different future and bringing back good news of what it might be like to live there.

Of course, the big picture has a past as well. In Christian thinking we call that 'the tradition'. Clergy are story-tellers and they have to understand, value and respect the story told by the past, for in that tradition is the huge accumulated wisdom of the Church and the millions of good and godly people who have made it up. The tradition is not set in stone, but nor is it set in plasticine. It has the strength and the malleability of living wisdom and needs to be appreciated and absorbed. What is true of the Church's total enterprise is also true of the local church. The priest as leader needs to understand the local story of the church and not to assume the old story books are now closed and he or she can write a whole new narrative. In the parishes I served I knew who carried the community story and who, therefore, I had to listen to in order to make sure I could place our new developments in a proper context. We all live in a continuing story; the new chapter has to move the story on, not abuse it.

Leaders set the direction

At one level Jesus' ministry looks to be a series of disconnected events, a ministry of odds and ends. He taught, healed, chatted on the road; he travelled a lot, enjoyed long conversational meals, had the occasional weekend break with friends; he prayed at night and early morning, took his disciples on retreat, worked hard with Peter, James and John. But where was the overall strategy, the five-year plan? Through the details, however, a simple strategy emerges – to live his ministry transparently under God and then take it to Jerusalem to put the challenge of it to the leaders there. There were three essential ingredients – *a quality of life, a key message, and a key location.*

Clergy leaders have a responsibility to take their interpretation of the larger cultural context (the big picture) and to discern collaboratively a local strategy for the church, built upon its *quality of life* and its *key message* about Jesus. Big thoughts are not enough; they have to be earthed in local strategies (a '*key location*') and in priorities that are consonant with the past, realistic about the present and open to God's future.

Here, then, we come to the crucial heart of priestly leadership: *the priest always leads in collaboration with others.* I'm always anxious when I hear curates saying they want to get on to having 'my own parish'. I understand the desire to make one's own mistakes but I fear the underlying mindset that the parish is a personal fiefdom. Ministry is always corporate. One of the most important re-alignments in recent years in our thinking about ministry has been the location of all ministry in baptism. Baptism is the commissioning of the people of God for their ministry in every place. Ministry therefore belongs first to Christ, then to his Body (through baptism into Christ), then to the Body's corporate leadership, and then to its servant – the priest. Jesus offered that model of servanthood not as a tactic if you can't get away with anything more robust, but as the paradigm for all Christian leadership (Mark 10.43–45). He also determined, right from the start, that he would work with a 'leadership team'. His first action, straight from the wilderness, was the calling together of his unlikely team. He knew he had to train the disciples and, within the larger group, to give special time to his core group of three. Of course there were times when he acted unilaterally. He 'set his face to go to Jerusalem'. That was his decision, not the result of consultation. But right until the cross he journeyed with others. And after the Ascension he left those others to get on with it (in the power of the Spirit).

There is no major endeavour undertaken in society today that is done alone. Everyone works in teams, whether they be GPs, teachers, social workers, business teams, design teams, sales teams – even the England football team on a good day! The Church's record is sadly mixed. Some tragically misplaced isolationism and competitiveness still bedevils (literally) the local church scene, particularly when clergy get together. Nevertheless, there has been a very encouraging move across the whole Church in the last generation to set up leadership teams, under a variety of names. Such teams offer an immediate multiplication of benefits in ideas, energy, prayer, personal support, division of work, sharing of pain and much more. Priests are team-leaders in this new world, but before that they are team-players, accepting responsibility to organize the team, hold it to account, and deftly arrange things to get the best out

*Another day with drunks, dropouts and deadbeats – how
he hated clergy chapter!*

of everyone. Indeed, perhaps it is best to think of a team as an
organism rather than a fixed entity, and thus something living
to enjoy.

Of course, teams don't just happen; they require prioritiz-
ing. It means that sometimes priests will not be able to do
the things they want to do or feel gifted to do because time,
thought, attention and prayer need to be poured into the
building of the team. This is not the place to go into any kind
of detail; other books do this (see Further resources section).
However, teams are usually helped by meeting regularly, often
fortnightly and no less than monthly. They benefit from
having real tasks, and members being trusted to get on with
their jobs and making mistakes if necessary. Teams flourish when
praying together is a first priority and a joy, not an option and
a duty. They are often helped by eating together and by the
wine flowing – moderately! Teams benefit from consultancy
and intentional training in self-awareness; the Myers-Briggs
Type Indicator and the Belbin classification of team roles are
useful tools to have in the bag. Teams often value going away
together to think, plan and pray, and maybe they remember the

old wisdom that human groups usually have to go through a process of forming, storming, 'norming' and performing before they reach the promised land of effective leadership.

It also salutary to remember that teams can be painful as well as productive. It should be some comfort to note that Jesus couldn't entirely handle his own team either. They vied for a place at the top table, arguing about who would be the greatest, they failed to understand him and asked silly questions, they denied even knowing him or they ran away. It was hardly an unqualified success story. But Jesus knew he had no other option but to work with this motley crowd of future leaders and martyrs. We are in the same position. The priest must not act alone.

And together, slowly, a vision and strategy will begin to emerge.

Leaders focus on people – including themselves

The role of the priest in the team and in the church as a whole is to do with people. In a previous generation the priest's task was described as 'picking people up, loving them, and letting them go'. This might sound a little patronizing today but the instinct is a sure one. People are to be loved. They aren't a means to an end. They are the glory of the Church, reflecting the glory of God because, as we know from Irenaeus, 'The glory of God is a human being fully alive.' The priest as leader, therefore, doesn't hide in the study, even if he or she is an introvert. The priest tries to develop the 'art of strategic presence' (see Chapter 9) and values the resulting relationships above all things.

In the leadership team inevitably the priest is *primus inter pares*, having been given responsibility for the mission and ministry in that place by the bishop. But that doesn't mean he or she has to chair the meetings or control the discussion. The priest brings his or her own gifts, supplemented by professional training and the particular knowledge and pastoral wisdom that comes from being at the heart of the community. However, the priest's main roles are to love and encourage the team, to motivate and mentor the members, to put in place support and training, to make sure the right people are in the right place, and to patrol the boundaries so that the team is relating properly to the wider Church and the decision-making bodies.

Whether in the leadership team or the wider Church, the priest as leader focuses on people. One of the main tasks is to thank people and affirm them in their Christian life and ministry. I once visited a church and went to thank the organist, who I knew had been a long-time servant at the organ console. She was clearly moved as she told me this was the first time she had ever really been thanked in 50 years. People grow when they are appreciated. It doesn't take much effort on our part but it makes a huge difference to individuals and ultimately to the atmosphere of a church.

The other person the priest has to focus on is himself or herself. It's been said that a leader without followers is just a person out for a walk, and there will be no followers if the leader isn't trusted. The most important element of leadership is character, and in Christian leadership that means character shaped by Christ. One writer identifies four of the key qualities as integrity, passion, curiosity and daring – all attributable to Christ. John Adair offers a daunting list – initiative, perseverance, integrity, humour, tact, compassion, efficiency, industry, audacity, honesty, self-confidence, justice, moral courage and consistency. Perhaps we might simply précis the list by looking at Jesus. (And it's interesting to note how many writers identify suffering as a key contributor to the humility needed by an effective leader. Jesus has been there too.) Christian leaders, therefore, need to develop emotional intelligence in addition to mental intelligence. If we add to that 'spiritual intelligence' we might be drawing a picture of Jesus, 'the pioneer and perfecter of our faith' (Hebrews 12.2). The perfect leader. Of course God also breaks the rules! God anoints unlearned and inexperienced people in a sophisticated and worldly culture to do what humanly speaking they could not do – from Moses onwards. Nevertheless the urgent needs of the contemporary Church point us towards some of those gifts noted above.

A word of warning: leadership can be lonely. It's been said that an individual's capacity for leadership is in direct proportion to his or her capacity to endure loneliness. Everyone has a view on the leader! There are colleagues, friends and family to understand and support, but the basic condition may still be there. Better to acknowledge it.

Two images

The priest is called to be a leader in mission. The role is unavoidable and exciting. When flying a plane only a few things are fatal – running out of fuel, flying too low, and going off course. In clergy leadership, running out of fuel is not having the spiritual energy we need and neglecting the absolute centrality of our life of prayer, scripture and sacrament. Flying too low is not keeping the vision high enough; aim low and we will surely succeed, but we will probably also crash. Going off course is failing to keep to priorities; a hundred distractions a day will seek to divert us; we have to know where we are going and keep on course. A final cause of crashes is said to be pilots simply forgetting to fly the plane when in a state of confusion or panic. Let the reader understand!

Another image is more positive. Christian leaders are like conductors of God's local orchestra. Our task is multi-layered. We have to interpret the music of the gospel to bring out all its rich textures and glorious melodies. We have ourselves to be students of the music, always learning, and sharing with the orchestra what both we and they have learned about this beautiful music. We have to help members of the orchestra to hear each other, to be aware of each other as they play their 'instrument' or use their gift. Without that sensitivity to each other both an orchestra and a church descend into a caco-phony of conflicting noises. And finally we have as conductors to share the risks of the performance with the orchestras we serve. Any live performance has about it the adrenalin-rushing potential for greatness, mere adequacy or total disaster.

Pray the Great Composer for the best performance we can ever imagine.

13

Attractive witness:
Pointing to Christ

The priest as evangelist

My fantasy is that somewhere in the world is a church that's so attractive it's irresistible. Then I want to put its DNA into a Petri dish, reproduce it, and give it to every gathering of God's people throughout the world. Sadly, I don't think such a church exists because every church is made up of imperfect human beings; but I remain convinced that this is the goal, because the most effective form of evangelism is a community living out the gospel so fully and attractively that people are drawn into its orbit and so discover Christ.

Mavis felt a strong calling to preach to the people of Tahiti

When the word 'evangelism' is used in a meeting of clergy you can immediately sense positions being taken up, and many of them are defensive. At a time when congregations in the Church in the West are declining, clergy are all too easily prone to guilt. A mass of cultural factors makes it very hard to achieve church growth and many priests would probably admit to themselves – but only to themselves – that they are really only trying to stem the losses. The word 'evangelism' just sends a shock of guilt through them.

On the other hand, all priests were in some sense 'evangelized' in order for them to find nothing else so attractive as being a Christian and no vocation so compelling as being a priest. The important move is to get behind the word 'evangelism' and offload the baggage that the word has accumulated. In any case, when evangelism is too self-conscious an activity it's often self-defeating. We live in a culture profoundly wary of spin, manipulation and hidden agendas. So evangelism as a sales pitch, a campaign, an argument, a presentation, or as proof or persuasion, is almost doomed to failure with the vast majority of people. A 'mission week' sends them diving for cover. But evangelism as making disciples, as friendship, conversation, invitation, challenge, participation, story-telling, pilgrimage – all this has much more resonance with our cultural preferences and (I would maintain) with the way of Jesus and the values of the gospel.

We also need to take account today of the *process* of coming to faith. It's much more likely to be on the gradual road to Emmaus rather than the dramatic road to Damascus. The more normal order of things is likely to be a first stage of 'blessing' where people are simply known and valued where they are, followed by a time simply of 'belonging' where they experience the life of the Christian community, but without commitment. This may lead to the birth of 'believing', not signing up to an entire package of doctrine but taking seriously the story and significance of the man called Jesus. And that in turn may lead to a new way of 'behaving' as the implications of Christian discipleship begin to make sense. Evangelism is simply the invitation to stay on that journey.

The priest has a particularly complex path to find through his or her own thinking and emotions and those of the church he or she serves. There are no certain rules to follow in our complex social environment. Changes in the cultural landscape are happening too quickly for us to assimilate them all. People talk about the demise of the Christian 'metanarrative', although it would be more accurate to talk of the demise of the metanarrative of Christendom as a world-view. (You might actually say that we live not only in a post-Christendom culture but also one that is post-secular. Religion and spirituality are back on the field, though not in a way that makes it easy for Christians to engage.) But in the midst of this confusion the call of the Ordinal is still clear: priests are to 'search for God's children in the wilderness of this world's temptations, and to guide them through its confusions, that they may be saved through Christ for ever'. As is always the case, priests don't do this alone. 'With all God's people,' we are told, 'they are to tell the story of God's love.' It's the privilege of every baptized Christian and nothing would give today's priests more pleasure than to tell the story of God's love and to see it being effective. The problem is how to do it.

The scale of the challenge

One of our defensive strategies is to argue that numerical growth isn't important; what matters is the quality of our church life. It must certainly be true that numbers alone can never be the sole criterion of success for those who follow a man who was crucified. But that argument misses the point. The gospel has always been concerned with both personal and social transformation; two sides of the same coin. If the number of people transformed by the Spirit of God and identifying with the Church falls too low, then the resources of the Church to be agents of social change will cease to be sufficient. The voice of the Church will disappear from the land as its increasingly elderly energies are employed in keeping its antiquated machinery from collapse. How then can God's Kingdom come if there aren't enough of God's people to make the bricks for him to use?

It's commonly agreed today that some 20 per cent of the population of Britain are either regular or irregular attenders at church. A further 40 per cent once had some connection with the church, a percentage equally split between those who could be interested once again and those who were so damaged by the experience that they want nothing more to do with it. The remaining 40 per cent have had virtually no experience of the church and are either mystified by it or find it completely irrelevant to their lives. Moreover, religion itself is often seen as part of the problem. Bono, lead singer of U2, said in an interview:

> I often wonder if religion is the enemy of God. It's almost like religion is what happens when the Spirit has left the building. God's Spirit moves through us and the world at a pace that can never be constricted by any one religious paradigm. The Spirit is described in the Holy Scriptures as much more anarchic than any established religion credits.

People have come increasingly to separate religion and spirituality. Church is perceived as either damaging or irrelevant. It represents a bygone age, and if it tries to preach Good News it comes across like a radio announcer telling us about a deep depression off Iceland.

The cultural ground appears to be rock hard, and into this harsh landscape steps the brave priest, believing with all his or her heart that Christ is the world's true light. It may help the priest to remember that the situation is hardly less promising than it was for 11 men and an unknown number of supporters on the day of Pentecost. The task was enormous and the odds against success were terrifying – except for the love of God, the presence of Christ, and the power of the Spirit. If a priest is inclined to batten down the hatches and hope to survive until retirement then here is the antidote. 'Telling the story of God's love' is in the title deeds of the Church. It's what the Church of God perceived to be its chief task right from the start. But (and this is the key point) evangelism happened *naturally*. It happened as spontaneously as light emanating from the sun, and it came from a *community* of believers who lived in the immediacy of God's presence.

Whatever style of evangelism the Church employs in the future it has to take account of the range of religious and non-religious backgrounds from which people come. There's no 'one-size-fits-all' evangelism. Those who make up the church's fringe may respond to more innovative and imaginative worship. Those who once attended but have drifted away may respond to relational evangelism in genuine friendships, and to good quality introductory and nurture courses. Those with minimal experience of church may be attracted by the quality of community and its engagement with the all-round needs and interests of ordinary people. Those who have been damaged by church in their earlier lives may be moved by genuine apology and dialogue. We look for a mixed economy of evangelism and for a range of Christian communities, some living 'inherited church' really well, and some pushing out into fresh ways of expressing gospel life.

And in the middle of this maelstrom stands the priest, trying to discern the signs of the times and the nudge of the Spirit in his or her locality. What might be an appropriate style of 'telling the story of God's love' here and now? Who might be ready to listen and talk? Who might tell the story best? What changes in church life might be necessary and how would they be received? Meanwhile, the funerals don't stop coming in . . .

The distinctive community

Whatever style of evangelism is appropriate in the priest's particular context, one of the key resources is going to be the quality of the Christian community. Evangelism is most effective when it's a by-product of the holistic living out of the gospel by a Christ-centred community. It's the 'wow' factor again. If a community reflects the kindness, the questioning and the radical challenge of Jesus, people are likely to come and ask what's going on. They'll be intrigued and probably provoked into asking their own questions.

Some people talk about a 'new monasticism' or 'communities without walls' emerging through the crevices of our tired church life. This doesn't have to be esoteric; the principles apply to the local church as well as anywhere else. Brother Sam of the Franciscans said this:

> Monastic life may seem utterly out of tune with the spirit of our times, yet if we're entering another dark age it may be to the wisdom of such a way that the Church of today needs to turn. I sense that the renewal of both Church and society will come through the re-emerging of forms of Christian community that are homes of generous hospitality, places of challenging reconciliation and centres of attentiveness to the living God.

Note the three main ingredients; hospitality, social engagement, spiritual authenticity. These three components offer a demanding and exciting agenda to the local church and they are precisely the elements of many 'fresh expressions' of church community that are proving interesting and attractive to those for whom traditional church is a closed book. Such faith communities may gather around alternative worship or an 'on-the-edge' neighbourhood project or a network church in a city centre, but those ingredients are usually present in some way or other. The question for the priest and congregation in a church operating in inherited mode is how those elements can be present there too.

One of the key tasks of evangelism in our day, therefore, is the building of communities of grace where Christ is known and his life is shared in an unforced and generous way. Evangelism then becomes a natural spin-off from the authentic living of the Christian life in community. One of the greatest gifts the Church has to offer a confused world at present is how to live together in peace and hope. The tragedy, of course, is that so often the Church has nothing to teach the world in this way, except the need for penitence. The answer isn't so much 'must try harder' to live well, as 'must dig deeper' into the riches of the gospel. There's always so much more to receive.

The role of the priest in evangelism

Few priests, as few Christians generally, have the particular gift of being an evangelist. All Christians are witnesses and should be able 'to give a reason for the hope that is in them' (1 Peter 3.15), but that is different from being able to lead people explicitly to faith in Jesus Christ. However, in the new paradigm of evangelism which this chapter has been suggesting, every priest has much to contribute because every priest is set at the heart of a Christian community which can come to exemplify the life of the gospel. What then is the role of the priest?

First, the priest is a motivator of change in the life of the community. No church will change by itself. The priest tries to demonstrate (though perhaps not in these words) that missiology comes before ecclesiology, in other words, that 'the God of mission has a Church', not that 'the Church of God has a mission'. The latter approach means that mission is always seen as yet another activity, rather than being of the *esse* of the Church. This is the necessary fundamental shift in the self-understanding of the church at local as well as national level and needs to be tackled by priests and their leadership teams by leading, teaching and example.

Second, priests see their role clearly as builders and shapers of community. The aim is to build a community where people stop *attending* church and start *being* church. The priest's goal with the leadership team is to let God build a community of irresistible character whose most notable characteristic is love. Evangelism is then a natural phenomenon; it doesn't have to be forced. It's the experience of people beginning to find themselves wrapped up in the love of God through his people. A fundamental question for a priest to ask, therefore, is likely to be: 'Is this church worth joining?' When the church gathers most distinctly to be itself, whether in worship, fellowship or service, is there an infectious hospitality? Does the world around matter to people? Is God perceptibly in the midst? Overall, the experience of Christian community needs to be one that is *life-giving*. Too much church life today fails that test. Perhaps in this age of health and fitness the local church might think of itself as a 'spiritual health and fitness centre'. But then it has to be able to deliver.

Third, the priest will try to enter as fully as possible into what it means to be a disciple of Jesus Christ. If it isn't happening for the priest, it may not be happening for others. At its best the transparency of the priest's experience is infectious. The collect for the day when the Church commemorates the saintly Bishop Edward King says: 'God of peace, who gave such grace to your servant Edward King that whomever he met he drew to Christ: fill us, we pray, with tender sympathy and joyful faith, that we also may win others to know the love that passes knowledge . . .' Every priest would surely be delighted if whoever he met he drew to Christ. It takes us back to the centrality of living close to Christ ourselves and daily renewing that transforming friendship. It's also worth remembering that people often judge the product by the spokesperson. The

German philosopher Nietzsche said of Jesus that 'his followers ought to look more redeemed'. What does our public image say about the vitality of our faith? What is our *life* saying?

There are, then, many things for the priest to attend to in helping the Christian community to be vibrant and attractive – creative, enriching worship; healthy, welcoming hospitality; relationships in which the story of faith can be shared naturally; genuine care for the wider community; accessible nurture courses; a risk-taking, adventurous church programme, and so on. However, the heart of a healthy Christian community is more elusive. It comes from a single-minded fascination with the mystery of God. As everyone is encouraged to look towards the sun so the people of God become sun-tanned and glowing with health, and this in turn draws others to 'come and see' (John 1.39). When people encounter a fuller demonstration of what it is to be human, they usually want to know more. They may not agree with the arguments we make but they can't disagree with the lives they see. The priest is called to be a person with such a life, and a begetter of that life in others.

As far as the Kingdom of God is concerned and the completion of God's new world, the end is not in doubt. All things will be gathered up in Christ, things in heaven *and things on earth* (Ephesians 1.10). That much is fine. What is less clear is how the Church in this generation can best contribute to the purposes of God. But we can be sure that our primary calling is to hold fast to the magnetic figure of Jesus Christ, around whom the future revolves, and to build communities of distinctive character around him. The rest is happily up to God.

14

Faith coach:
Helping people to grow

─────◆◆◆─────

The priest as teacher

'The average Christian is as well equipped to meet an aggressive atheist or agnostic as a boy with a peashooter is to meet a tank.' It's a line I read long ago and it's stayed with me because I fear it may be at least partially true. I comfort myself with the thought that someone with an experience is never at the mercy of someone with an argument. Nevertheless, because I believe the Christian faith is about truth as well as about experience, I don't want Christians to come across as fluffy thinkers who haven't really understood the problems.

It's impossible not to make comparisons with the adherents of other faiths. There is a robust seriousness about the way young Muslims and Jews learn the traditions and teachings of their faith. Study is part of the deal. Television pictures of mosques always seem to show them packed with young men, and the assumption must be that their faith matters to them. They take it seriously. Worrying questions afflict me: does the understanding of the average Christian believer match any of this? Does our Christian maturity as church members sufficiently keep pace with the maturity of our years? If we're prepared to put so much effort into becoming computer-literate, why do we put so little effort into becoming faith-literate? Or, to be particular, how many Christians would have been able to respond convincingly to the fanciful ideas of Dan Brown's best-selling novel, *The Da Vinci Code*?

The priest has the task and the pleasure of enabling the baptized people of God to grow into Christian maturity. In a sense it doesn't matter how people have come into the household of faith. They may have grown up in it, with all the benefits of familiarity and stability. They may have encountered the rich sacramental food of Anglo-Catholic devotion. They may have had the transforming experience of meeting Christ in a lively evangelical setting. They may have swung into faith through a charismatic festival or wandered into a silent church at sunset. The route into faith doesn't matter – as long as we then grow. There's a lifetime of fascinating discovery ahead as we explore the infinite riches of Christ. Paul, as ever, sets the bar high. The goal is that 'all of us come to the unity of the faith and of the knowledge of the Son of God, to maturity, *to the measure of the full stature of Christ*' (Ephesians 4.13). He gives a reason for this: 'We must no longer be children, tossed to and fro and blown about by every wind of doctrine and by people's trickery' (v. 14). The goal is a noble one. The priest's problem, however, is likely to be that of motivating people for the journey.

There's another darker reason why attention to the maturity of the Church is important. The world's future is, in a sense, quite fragile. The Government's Chief Scientific Adviser has put the world's chances of survival in a recognizable form to the end of the century at about 50:50. There are constant wars and rumours of wars, and the possibility of biological terrorism on an unimaginable scale. Climate change may now be irreversible, with untold consequences. Nanotechnology could take a wrong turn and result in the meltdown of much that we take for granted. In this context of high uncertainty, if darkness does in fact fall, would our faith be ready for it or would that faith crumble? We should need faith more than ever, but would it sustain us? It's interesting that the trilogy of films *The Lord of the Rings* has been so popular. Perhaps people sense the truth of the epic's deep mythology about innocence and evil, about the dark forces emanating from Mordor, about struggle and sacrifice and survival. Faced with these possibilities being acted out in the real world, are Christians still to be found playing in the Shire?

Even at a more imaginable, human level, how equipped are any of us to face the darkness of overwhelming personal tragedy? We see it on the television news (before it moves on to the sport) and think it will never happen to us. But it does, and many a Christian faith has been broken because the simplicities of belief could not withstand the overwhelming assault of suffering. 'Why did God allow this to happen?' are the last words they say as they close the church doors behind them. Priests have a job on their hands.

The Church as a learning community

One of the dimensions of the Church which we have been recovering in recent years has been that of the local church as a learning community. In the heart of the community, Christ is the Teacher, as he was in his embryonic church in the Upper Room. 'You call me Teacher and Lord – and you are right, for that is what I am' (John 13.13). Every local church should be a school for Christian maturity. In any school there is both formal and informal learning, and so too in the church people grow up into Christ through being part of the rough and tumble of community life, testing behaviour, listening and learning, worshipping and trying to pray, arguing and being reconciled, serving and stumbling – the whole gamut of life together. We're learning about being a Christian all the time we belong to the community, which is why Jesus' image of him being the Vine and believers being the branches is so apposite (John 15.5). The sap of the Vine runs through the branches all the time, bringing them to health and maturity. It follows that, 'apart from me you can do nothing'. Christ is the Teacher

The Revd Horace Chesnutt told Class 2 about the Ascension

at the heart of the community upon whose life and wisdom we depend.

However, the priest is one of Christ's teaching assistants. Some priests don't see themselves as being up to the task. They are aware, perhaps, of having had only two or three years' theological education and look with some embarrassment at their lack of reading since. They're aware of skating on thin ice when preparing a sermon or answering questions at an adult confirmation group. There are two answers to this lack of confidence. One is that it's never too late to start reading again. The other is that every priest knows more than he or she thinks, and more (theologically) than nearly everyone in the congregation. Again, however, this is a shared task and there are those in the congregation who are well able to lead groups in learning about discipleship and who bring teaching and learning skills as well as commitment to their faith.

Just as important as what the priest knows is how he or she helps people to learn. Educational method is crucial. I remember a Reader who had been asked to lead a Lent group. He stood in the corner of the living room and gave a fairly garbled 45-minute lecture. I guarantee very little was learned. When I taught in a theological college four former students were asked to return and talk about their first year or two's experience. One wise current student asked them what they now wished they had received more preparation for, while at college. Each one replied unequivocally that they wished they had learned more about adult education.

Most of the methods and skills are really quite straight-forward. People learn best by being able to identify their own questions and participate in their own learning. Engaging people's imagination with the issue, giving input in small bites with opportunity to respond, working in pairs or small 'break-out' groups, reinforcing the spoken word with visual material, posing problems for the group to work on, using DVD clips, paintings and literature – there are many skills any teacher would gladly pass on to a priest willing to learn.

A very important quality for the priest as Christ's teaching assistant is humility. It's so refreshing to hear a public figure say, 'I don't know – but I'll find out.' The priest doesn't need to have all the answers; indeed people can become weary of one who does, because they know that some at least of what he or she is so confident about must be bluff, and even if it isn't it's unlovely. The church is a community of learners, and that includes the priest. Priests need to show that they also take growing and learning in the Christian life seriously, that they also go on courses, read constantly, go on retreat, above all that they *think*, and talk to Christ about their thinking. Moreover, we need another, deeper, type of humility as Christian learners, and that is humility before mystery. Not all questions can be resolved; some just need to be deepened, like the nature of the Trinity or the puzzle of evil and suffering. We don't help our communities to grow by passing on the Christian faith in neat packages of pre-digested doctrine. Nor do we help by keeping people playing happily in the shallow end when the bigger rewards are really to be found at the deep end. We may be more helpful if we open up profound issues of life and faith, lay out a map, say where we've travelled on our own journey, and invite people to explore for themselves.

It's important, therefore, that priests in their role as 'faith coaches' don't inflate their own importance and abuse their power by trying to produce clones who replicate their own carefully honed view of what a faithful Christian looks like. Every faith journey must be allowed its own uniqueness both in overall design and in detail. The priest can provide a goal, some suggested routes and some provisions to put into the back-pack but he or she must never insist that there's only one right path for learning and growth. One of the exciting things about these journeys is that there are no right, and not many wrong, sets of choices to be made, like some godly maze where a 'wrong' decision at one point negates the whole journey. Whatever choices we make God will take and use, offering a different set of possibilities depending on which way we have journeyed thus far. He has a vision for us rather than a set plan.

Learning and connecting

It's worth remembering that Jesus was a lay person. He was not a priest and indeed, although he remained a Jew, he had a fairly uncomfortable relationship with the priests of his faith community. The lay status of Jesus may encourage today's priests to take with the utmost seriousness the vocation of lay people as witnesses in the everyday world. A priest was once asked how many ministers he had in his team. 'Eighty,' he replied, 'but only one of us is paid.' The priest's task isn't to capture talented lay people and domesticate them to the inner world of the church, to make them into chief servers. It's to equip them to bear witness to Christ in the midst of the complexities of their various worlds – of work, family, leisure pursuits and so on – as well as in the various dimensions of their lives – relationships, money, sex, ambition, loyalties, commitments and so on. The clergy's task is to help and encourage the people of God accurately to describe the experience of being in the world and trying to change it. To put it at its highest, Christian laity are God's new humanity in the world, where God is already at work, and they are present there not just in pastoral mode but, more deeply, engaging the principalities and powers in the name of Christ. Lay people are on the front line; the clergy's task is to offer all the support they can.

The teaching task of the priest, therefore, is to provide access to knowledge *and to help people make connections*. These two aspects are inseparable. You have to have some appropriate theological knowledge in order to have anything to connect to everyday life, but without making connections knowledge can become simply a deposit of miscellaneous facts. The best learning courses, therefore, are committed to both knowledge and connectedness, but usually they leave the second to local implementation. Often the most useful questions come in short packets. I knew one teacher whose favourite question after a student had expounded some topic at length was, 'So what?' Meaning, 'What use can you make of that? How does that tie in to everyday life?' Similarly, E. M. Forster's aphorism 'only connect' is a valuable slogan for every priest to practise. Our preaching and teaching ought always to have that goal, to help connect the riches of the Christian faith with the pressing dilemmas of people's everyday issues at work, at home, in the school, office, boardroom and shopfloor. In ordinary pastoral conversations the priest might also ask 'connecting' questions such as: 'Where do you think God might be in all that?' 'What might be the Christlike thing to do there?' Only connect.

Some sort of educational programme ought to be available in every church in the land, even if it's only a matter of encouraging people to take advantage of what's available somewhere else through deanery and diocesan courses and parish partnerships. Every church would benefit from an access course by which people can begin exploring Christian faith and life. The field is getting quite crowded with Alpha, Emmaus,

Credo, Christianity Explored, Start and others. There may need to be a stage even before that – questions and answers in a pub, or a group for 'no-holds-barred' discussion. The priest and leadership team might think hard about what form of small groups would work best in their church, whether cells, or home groups of limited duration, or special interest groups focusing on art, music, poetry or film. There can be day and weekend conferences, town-wide Adult Christian Education (ACE) programmes, diocesan courses for discipleship and ministry, and national opportunities too, not least in the plethora of festivals now on offer – Spring Harvest, New Wine, Greenbelt, Soul Survivor, Walsingham.

And books. Every priest has a library and the judicious loan of a book to someone at the right time can bring innumerable benefits, not least the possibility of an entire journey into Christian learning. One priest used to have a range of relevant books available for loan at every educational event in the parish. When he left the parish after eight years he found that he had lent out over a thousand books in that period. This would not be the case in every parish, of course, but the principle holds: there are more riches in accessible Christian literature than most Christian people dream of. Alongside books, however, we also need to be aware of appropriate learning styles for non-book cultures. Many such materials and methods are home grown and fully contextualized, but it's important to remember how intimidating the literary culture of the Church can seem to be to many people.

Not just the mind

If we are to grow into the full stature of Christ we can't only be talking about the life of the mind and the ability to make connections between faith and everyday life. We must even more be talking about the life of the spirit – spiritual intelligence as well as mental intelligence. This was considered in Chapter 3 as we explored the role of the priest in helping people to grow in prayer and love of God. This needs to be the underlying context of all our 'faith coaching'. There is sometimes an unreality about people's Christian living because they have never really discovered the intimacy with God that makes it all add up. Without that central 'locking nut' the whole Christian enterprise will fail to hold together. Nothing is more important therefore than helping people to find wells of living spiritual water through which the grace of Christ can flood the soul. Then the aphorism 'only connect' comes into its own, because the only connection that really matters has fallen into place.

This chapter has emphasized the use of the mind because of the often superficial understanding of faith in a Church that has become too used to its established position in Western society and cultural life. The pressure is now on to live the faith more deeply and with more understanding. The most important growth for any Christian, however, is growth in the knowledge and love of Christ. People may labour at large concepts and ideas but nevertheless possess a deep wisdom of the heart that has come from following the Christian way day in, day out, for years. It's the fruit of the Spirit (Galatians 5.22–25) that brings joy to the heart of God and this is where the principles in Chapter 3 about prayerful discipleship become urgent. 'For to me, living *is* Christ,' said St Paul in one of his most pregnant phrases (Philippians 1.21), and that is surely one profound description of our ultimate goal.

Christian maturity is an unfinished life-long task, but the goal is not only noble, it's essential if we are to survive the battering of twenty-first-century life. The process is exciting and full of discovery, and it makes the priest realize afresh that, for all of us, to be alive is to be a learner.

15

Mature risk-taker:
Thinking outside the box

━━━━━●━◆━●━━━

The priest as pioneer

I have a cartoon that shows a man and his cat looking together at a tray of cat litter. The man is saying sternly to the
cat, 'Never, ever, think outside the box.' That may be fine for
the cat, but not for us in the Church of God in these days. Radical thinking is no longer a luxury and no priest is immune
from the challenge of re-thinking the Church's ministry.

Some things remain recognizably the same. Priests still live
in vicarages and lead services in churches; they take baptisms
and weddings (increasingly in that order) and most of the community's funerals; they chair PCCs and sit on the governing
bodies of local schools. Parish priests are normally guaranteed
a monthly stipend, a house until retirement and a non-
contributory pension (although this job security has recently
begun to slip alarmingly for the first time). Nevertheless, at
a deeper level the ground is shifting. The parish system is
stretched to the limit; money is running out; the age of congregations is rising sharply – project many ageing congregations
20 years on and few people may be left in the pews. We don't
need to list the social and spiritual changes that are causing the
tectonic plates to grind together increasingly noisily. They are
well known and probably irreversible.

The consequence of these major cultural and ecclesial
changes is that today's priests may be ministers of the last rites

of the Church as we know it. There will be sorrow in this, of course, but at the same time God is bigger than all our structures and each expression of church has its season. We can thank God for the gift of the past and trust him for the future. Of course there will be continuity in forms of church as well, and the principles of priestly ministry that we have been exploring in this book will find their expression in whatever form of church emerges in the future. However, the *context* of this ministry will be very different, which is why the priests of today and tomorrow need to be able to think outside the conventional church box. The situation is the more complex because today's priests need to be living in two ecclesial worlds at the same time. It's as if the ship has to undergo a refit while still at sea; it can't retreat to dry dock and take time out. We have to do the future thinking for the Church while the former model is still just about surviving because, if we leave it too long, the 'catch-up' distance becomes too great.

Living in two realities

Of all people, priests shouldn't be afraid of living in two realities. It's what we do all the time. We live in the overlap of the human dimension ('earth') and the divine dimension ('heaven'). We live in the 'between times' where the Kingdom of God has come and yet is still expected. We live in a sacramental world where ordinary things assume extraordinary meanings. All Christians are experienced in living in several dimensions at the same time. So the priest has many resources for living in parallel, interlocking worlds.

This means that as ministers of the last rites for some traditional forms of church we must be careful not to bully or blame congregations unable to make the changes that the future may be requesting or requiring. The priest has to either help them revive (or rather, be resurrected), or to provide palliative care as they come to a natural end. No priest comes into ordained ministry to help congregations close their churches but some-times it may be a deeply priestly task to sit by the deathbed, walk alongside the bereaved and be a presence of continuous hope looking to the risen Christ.

There's another key theological truth to be explored here and that's to do with losing one's life. We can never save our own life as a Church, but have to be prepared to lose it and lay it down so that it's available to God, whatever God wants to do with it. This means turning away from the Church as an institution and turning towards God and the world. It may even be that as the Church-as-it-has-been is humiliated and powerless it will truly become the Body of Christ to which people turn for healing. People may at last recognize the Christ they truly need.

'Turning away from the Church as an institution' needs to be carefully understood. It doesn't mean throwing in the towel. It means, rather, focusing on the things that really mat-ter (God and the world) and letting the shape of the Church be re-configured around the new realities God is presenting to us, rather than the realities to which we tried to be faithful in a previous age. Today's church leaders in diocese and parish are therefore unavoidably engaged in the hard thinking and pray-ing necessary to re-design the Church. But 'losing our life' means that nothing is sacrosanct – except the gospel itself. All this can be very unnerving for a priest who just wants to get on with the job of loving God and serving his people. There is little in ministry today that causes more stress to clergy than having to live in the two realities at the same time, re-imagining the Church for tomorrow while still having to minister in the Church of today, the demands of which don't decrease to allow time for the new work to get started. This kind of dual-thinking may be deeply disturbing and turn a priest's mind longingly to the day of his or her pension. The more hopeful response, how-ever, is to go deeper into the transforming paradigm of death and resurrection at the heart of the Christian faith. This is no mere theological plaything; it's the reality by which we need to live, and it enables us still to rejoice and celebrate the love of God, even in the midst of much uncertainty.

Design principles for a new Church

The shape of the Church to come is not at all clear as yet, but what we do have is certain design principles emerging from the mist. There are a number of underlying moves for the Church and its clergy to make.

From individual ministry to a community of ministers in mission

God never made us to be alone but the clergy have sometimes had a good go at it! The days when we could afford rivalry and jealousy are over. Indeed, they never existed. Clergy and laity need to work together in teams and partnerships, enjoying the wide range of skills and insights, relaxed in their own contribution to the whole, and benefiting from the support, help and comfort each receives from the others. We flourish when we work and pray in an atmosphere of trust and respect, seasoned with humour and fun. It isn't always easy, but the goal of healthy teamwork is worth every ounce of effort. Every ministry I've had in the last 30 years has involved me working in a team, constantly correcting my isolationist tendencies and offering me much greater wisdom than I would ever have managed myself.

From guarding boundaries to growing relationships

Territory, in the sense of parish boundaries, is not important to a society that exists increasingly in networks. Equally unimportant are the mental boundaries that clergy sometimes set up against 'them' (usually the diocese or the bishop). We live in a relational society, and in any case we have a core trinitarian theology that places relationship at the heart of our self-understanding as a Church. What will be increasingly important is a 'bottom-up' approach to mission with local expressions of church life being trusted to make decisions about priorities, personnel, buildings and finance. Reciprocally, clergy called to ministries of oversight need to be trusted and not suspected of malice. We really are all on the same side! In this context of trust and respect new forms of church should be able to flourish – and sometimes fail – but, either way, to be owned and supported by the whole Church.

From partial ministry to holistic mission

Like all organizations, when a church is under pressure it tends to retreat into domesticity. It's easier to arrange the summer fayre and reorganize the area under the tower than to engage with the needs of the community or start a new service for spiritual seekers. The result is that many churches have become seriously lop-sided in their ministry, taking on more of the characteristics of a religious club than an open community serving the neighbourhood in the name of Christ. The mission of the Church is like a pair of scissors with the two blades representing evangelism and social action. Both blades tend to become rusty if the scissors are kept in a drawer. Both blades are needed in holistic mission. More and more churches are asking basic questions about the core purpose of the church and many are finding that when churches act together in partnership the opportunities for active mission on all fronts are greatly multiplied, and God's love is shown to be practical and life-giving. The key move is from self-interest to serious service. Through events organized by Soul Survivor, and others like the North-East's NE1, for example, young people have shown how gardening, cleaning up parks and running football festivals can rejuvenate holistic mission. Local clergy have been delighted.

From Sunday faithful to weekday disciples

This is the move from attending church to being the church. The process will never be complete because people come to church for all sorts of idiosyncratic reasons and must always be made welcome, but increasingly the message is getting across that what really matters is the 167 hours of the week that Christians are *not* in church. Churches are increasingly intent on making disciples rather than collecting Sunday worshippers, and the enthusiasm of many lay people who are discovering the riches of a living, world-related theology is a joy to the priest and to the angels of God. The After Sunday project based at Durham Cathedral, for example, encourages large numbers of Christians to hold Sunday and Monday together, in part through its imaginative website.

From delegated ministry to shared ministry

Clergy are learning that delegation is not enough. Delegation keeps all the strings firmly in clerical hands and causes immense frustration to able lay people. Shared ministry starts from the assumption of collaboration, not domination, and enables all God's people to exercise their gifts. Theoretically the priest has only to rejoice at all this. In practice there is an even more important role for him or her as the one who oversees and deploys the plethora of gifts and enthusiasms – and copes with the mistakes. But at least the cauldron is bubbling and not stagnant.

From autonomy to accountability

The priest has traditionally been a law unto himself and to God, with the occasional nod in the direction of the bishop. The house and stipend have been assured and with a bit of fast foot-work and stubbornness he or she could avoid interference from people such as archdeacons and bishops. (In George Eliot's *Middlemarch* Mrs Cadwallader, the vicar's wife, complains of her husband, 'He will even speak well of the bishop, though

I tell him it's unnatural in a beneficed clergyman. What can you do with a husband who attends so little to the niceties?') That culture is fast disappearing and the clearest sign of this is the way that ministerial review is moving from being an optional personal development review to a performance-based appraisal. There are clearly things to watch out for here. The Church is not a business. The goal is not sales and profits. Our currency is the love of God, not the money markets. Nevertheless the move towards personal accountability is something the world has rightly taught the Church, because authority without accountability is always dangerous. (Even Jesus was accountable to his Father.) With wise changes, however, the Church of the future can hope to be more purposeful and effective in the service of the Kingdom and clergy may feel more supported in a culture of both transparency and accountability.

From conventional faith to passionate commitment

Increasingly, being involved with a church is a positive choice, not an accident. This means that conventional, un-tested and little-exercised faith is giving way to intentional and serious faith. Propositional truth, which people can either take or leave, is proving, not surprisingly, to be less satisfactory to people than a transforming encounter with Jesus Christ. People are increasingly suspicious of packages of truth passed on in unreconstructed ways from generation to generation. They look for the evidence of transformed lives. The Church is recovering the power of testimony and emphasizing the importance of converting friendships. Ours is a 'seeing is believing' culture and the gospel is effective when it is written in people's lives. As a bishop who takes many confirmations I can vouch for the rejuvenating effect on the service (and on me!) of personal stories which earth the liturgy in the reality of lives made new. Of course, spiritual experience can't be the whole measure of a church's effectiveness but it has to be a minimum gift to worshippers or they won't return. This may be the lasting legacy of charismatic renewal which has been well integrated into the mainstream of the Church's life.

From self-preservation to suffering and celebration

The Church in the West has had it its own way for too long. It's now entering a period of much more gritty reality, which will be marked by both suffering and celebration. It seems that, in his mercy, God has reminded us that what we are handling is a lively, explosive gospel, not an optional accessory. The road ahead may be risky but it will be infinitely more interesting than we have allowed it to be in the past. Stories from linked churches around the world have inspired Christians to learn, pray and give. There is also a growing appetite for celebratory events, festivals, cathedral services and so on, demonstrating that praise is often the Church's best response to times of trial.

New shapes for the Church

This is where the crystal ball gets cloudy. Certain principles may be emerging but how they will shape the Church of the future is still in negotiation, and, in a time when change is the only constant, the negotiations will probably never end. However, some distinctive shapes seem to be looming out of the mist. One is the prospect of a mixed-economy Church. Where traditional church is well led there continues to be huge potential for growth, more so in fact than in most of the more fragile fresh expressions of church. Welcoming churches with imaginative worship, intentional about community and centred on Christ, with skilled, sensitive leadership and a real commitment to the well-being of the neighbourhood, are still growing strongly. But they need to be balanced by risk-taking ventures into emerging forms of church – mid-week congregations, after-school church, youth congregations, community projects, networks based on alternative worship, the internet or Starbucks – all these need to be owned and trusted by the whole Church and not just left to enthusiasts. The Church needs to be a truly mixed economy.

A second emerging shape for tomorrow's Church is the larger units of collaboration going under a variety of names around the country, among them clusters, mission areas and localities. They offer greater flexibility and imaginative possibilities for mission and ministry as well as the advantages of scale and personal support, but they depend as ever on the positive commitment of each priest and parish. Ecumenical possibilities are legion as long as they aren't just seen as a complication.

The third emerging shape is that of the 'resource church', a new incarnation of the old 'minster'. A resource church does as the title suggests: it resources outlying ecclesial communities from the wider range of its own strengths in people, facilities, training and finance. A staff team in such a church might consist of priests with specialist gifts (training, spirituality, commercial chaplaincy, etc.), a youth minister, Readers and self-supporting ministers, an administrator, perhaps a music director, and others. They would be part of a wider team of able lay people all of whom would be available to resource the dispersed smaller churches in the locality, which may be meeting in a well-established church, a school or a living room, depending on the need. The dispersed churches could be more provisional in character and they would not all need to try and be 'big churches', with every aspect of ministry offered improbably in every place (as at present). Collegiality and flexibility would be written into this resource-church model, but the journey to them from the present position of independent local empires might be a tough one.

What sort of priests?

Does all that has been said about the future Church imply that we need a different kind of priest? Well, yes and no. No, because the priestly gifts and skills outlined in this book are essentially transferable. We need good and godly priests who are wise in the priestly arts and adaptable in terms of context. On the other hand the uncertainties and risks of the future mean that people will need to do much heart-searching before they offer themselves for the exciting ministries of the years ahead. The Church of England has identified the need for a new category of lay or ordained 'pioneer minister', but every priest will need to have some of this pioneering spirit in his or her soul. The one disabling characteristic will be rigidity. The one necessity will be holiness. Candidates will need to be both humble and confident in facing the bishop's awesome question: 'Do you believe that God is calling you to this ministry?'

16

Flower arranger:
Managing the church's life

The priest as manager

There is considerable and understandable resistance to the idea of the priest as a manager. It seems to imply the crudest functional understanding of the role of a priest, collapsing the notion of 'being' into simply 'doing'. In a culture obsessed with outcomes and rushing ever faster from one activity to another, the priest stands for an alternative set of values in which human life is precious even if not productive. Those who are powerless in society through social disadvantage, disability, mental illness or other difficulties need to be assured that economic productivity is not the only measure of worth. The priest is a reminder of another Presence and a different value-framework, not because of any particular virtue in him or her, but through the priest's symbolic identity, which introduces new criteria into a community's life. Justice, mercy, compassion, generosity, forgiveness – these are the sort of qualities the priest is supposed to represent, without even saying a word. Priests also embody a different passage through life, with prayer, stillness, recollection and reflection woven into the fabric of their being. None of this is helped by the description of the priest as a manager.

However, certain things have to be done in the life of the local church if it is to bear witness to Christ. Services have to be held; people have to be cared for; Parochial Church

Councils have to meet; the dead have to be buried; the story of God's love has to be told; the parish share has to be paid, and so on. The priest is the one charged by the bishop with overseeing the good ordering of the church's life, and oversight implies organization. It is this activity with which we are now concerned, whatever the description of it. I have chosen the image of flower arranging not because I have a particular fascination with that mysterious art but because it illustrates that there are hordes of ordinary activities that somehow have to be organized. They don't just happen by chance. Moreover, if all the 'flowers' of the church's life are well arranged – the gifts discerned, the ministries deployed – the impact for the Kingdom of God is greatly enhanced, and may even be a thing of beauty.

Leadership and management

We have already explored the role of the priest as a leader and touched on the difference between leadership and management. Essentially, leaders watch the horizon and set the direction, focusing their energies on motivating and encouraging the people for whom they have responsibility, while managers have to do the detailed planning and organize the resources, focusing their energies on processes and problem-solving. Leaders envision and motivate change while managers handle the resulting complexity.

Nevertheless, this purity of theory often breaks down in the heat of everyday ministry. Or in my case, the wet. I had just gone to a parish to serve as a vicar for the first time and it was a wet, cold Sunday night. I discovered that somebody had to pull the dustbins a considerable distance from behind the church hall to the main road for emptying the following morning. As I struggled through the cold, wet night after a hard first Sunday I remember muttering darkly about the right use of a priest's time and effort, and promising myself there was a better way. I was, of course, both right and wrong. It was a good reminder of my role as a servant who shouldn't be standing on his fragile dignity, but I was also right that there was a better way of fulfilling this chore. It was a matter of organization.

I once entered a priest's study and was rendered speechless by a vision of complete chaos. The floor was piled high with mound after mound of books, papers, reports, bills, minutes, telephone directories, shopping lists and unopened letters. The rumour of a desk being located somewhere in the midst of this disaster area could not be corroborated. The priest was routinely apologetic but otherwise unabashed. I knew him to be a learned and much loved priest so I'm clear that inefficiency is not incompatible with godliness, but I couldn't help reflecting on how much more valuable that priest's ministry could have been with a modicum of organization. There are other cases, however, where it seems that such a chaotic study is indeed the outward and visible sign of inward and spiritual clutter.

As ministry becomes more demanding and complex I believe the time has come when proper parish administrative support is no longer a luxury but has now become a necessity for every priest. It should be non-negotiable and every priest ought to have it guaranteed before taking on a new post. I remember the huge relief I felt when I first got a parish administrator. Suddenly everything fitted into place. The parish had a hub. Someone else was responsible for making sure that things happened, that people knew what they were supposed to know, that connections were made across the range of parish life. It was a major re-balancing of leadership, management and administrative roles and enabled me to focus on what I was called to do. (I no longer took out the bins!) There may well be resistance to the appointment of a parish administrator, and such a function can take many shapes, but best of all is one person, paid, with a clear job description, whole- or part-time, respected as a full member of the leadership team. Smaller parishes obviously need to adapt the model but the growth of united benefices, clusters, localities and mission areas means that full-time appointments are becoming more feasible.

Managing others

Clergy often lament the difficulty of working with volunteers. Authority is cloudy; there are no sanctions; you can be let down at short notice. It's well to remember that those who lead and manage commercial and other organizations often speak of similar constraints because the truth is that we are all dealing with the same complex, mysterious and unique reality called the human person. The Christian sees the stakes as being even higher – every person is made in God's image and is the object of God's love.

Priests are servants of the people of God, not masters (Mark 10.42–45). This kind of leadership requires relational skills of a high order, which to some come naturally and to others are the result of hard work and constant monitoring. However, there is no incompatibility between, on the one hand, being a servant leader utterly dependent on God's grace and, on the other, offering people with discrete tasks in the parish full job descriptions, clear lines of accountability and strong avenues of support. People usually respond to clarity and transparency, and they appreciate high levels of responsibility combined with high levels of support. The details of this can be found elsewhere (see Further resources section) but my concern here is with the principles of managing complex activity in the voluntary, relational culture of a church.

The same principles apply to the running of meetings. I once had to go to a series of meetings in which I almost lost the will to live. The chairing of the meetings was so loose as to be non-existent and the frustration levels were astronomical. The meetings in our church life belong to God and should be infused with God's presence both by the way prayer embraces them and the way the meeting is conducted. A balanced agenda, clarity about the status of each agenda item (report, discussion, decision), preparation by the Chair, clear introductions and conclusions, a known time-frame, participation – all these are obvious principles. It might be good to have a period of quiet reflection and prayer built into some discussions and a lit candle reminding everyone of the presence of the living Christ. By the end of a meeting we want people to feel that decisions were taken because 'it seemed good to the Holy Spirit and to us . . .' (Acts 15.28).

Personal management

In addition to the effective and efficient organization of the parish, the priest also has responsibility for his or her personal organization, particularly of time and work at the desk. This is not the book to offer detailed suggestions. Such books exist (see Further resources) but this one is mainly concerned with underlying principles. I offer five.

Regard administration as a pastoral exercise

Good administration is part of good pastoral care. Behind nearly every piece of paper on the desk is someone asking for a response, for help, for advice, for support. (I say 'nearly' because junk mail invites a different response, and spam email is equally dismissable.) It may even help to adapt our Lord's unequivocal statement to become, 'Whatever you do to the least of these pieces of paper, you do to me.' There is a person behind the paper and that person needs to be treated with respect.

Find a regime and keep to it

We all work in different ways. Some get to their desk early and try to clear it; others set aside a morning a week for administration. Some tackle their emails last thing at night; others pop in and out during the day. Some need a clear desk to have a clear mind; others have a more fluid, but nevertheless purpose-ful, approach to the movement of paper around the desk. The important principle is to find what works and to sustain that regime.

Make sure the important isn't chased out by the urgent

This is easier said than done. People don't have their crises accord-ing to the spaces in our diary. Nevertheless, simply asking the question is often enough. 'Is this really important or merely an urgent-sounding detail?' 'What are the truly important things that my place of ministry needs of me this week/month/year?' The danger is that things that are urgent but not important will chase away things that are important but not urgent.

Pass on all you can with a glad heart!

Priests have quite enough to do without doing things that someone else can quite easily or properly do. Whatever we can pass on or delegate we should do with alacrity and without guilt. Empowering others benefits us all. This also means respecting the proper domain of the administrator. Clergy aren't always good at knowing how to use an administrator properly because of the pastoral dimension of so much that happens, but a clear job description and good communication ought to help.

Always be trying to develop the gifts and skills of others

It's all very well the priest knowing in theory that he or she is not a 'one-man-band' in ministry, but this needs to translate into an intentional policy of developing the gifts and ministries of the whole people of God. All ministry grows out of the baptismal commissioning of God's people, entrusted together with the mission and ministry of Christ. Many priests still fall for the old half-truth 'it's easier to do it myself'. In the long run the church will only grow when the gifts of God's people are arranged into the glorious floral display that is their true potential. The priest as 'flower arranger' has a clear calling to identify, recruit, train, deploy, monitor and nurture the full ministerial workforce that God has given him or her. (Those six stages are all important.) It means focusing on fewer tasks and people in the short term but the opportunities created in the long term vastly outweigh the limitations.

On not blaming others

Everyone whose work puts them under pressure finds other people to blame. It's entirely understandable and those in more senior positions have to accept that dealing with people's projections is part of the job. Clergy too can find themselves projecting their frustrations on to 'the diocese', the PCC, the intransigent colleague, 'the Church'. All of this is safer than blaming God who may actually be the intended victim, for it's God who has called us into this mess and who doesn't seem to want to get us out. But subconsciously we know that God can't be blamed or all sorts of spiritual mayhem might result, so we find other targets. All this may be understandable but it isn't ultimately sensible or productive. A moment's thought brings the realization that the archdeacon isn't conducting a vendetta against us, that the Diocesan Secretary isn't sitting at his desk thinking up ways to be cussed, and that the bishop hasn't made a policy decision to renege on the gospel. In any case the archdeacon isn't a different person from the vicar he was in the neighbouring parish; he's still Michael, who loves God and longs for people to know and serve him. The Diocesan Secretary is doing an impossible job and having to pass on the consequences of an increasingly regulated and litigious society that affects the Church as much as any other body. The bishop more than anyone wants the priests of the diocese to flourish because he knows their enjoyment and satisfaction in ministry is crucial if the Kingdom is to grow.

The more measured response of the priest therefore is to stand shoulder to shoulder with every other Christian in the diocese, and look towards God in trust and hope. Sniping at each other has never been a successful strategy in any army, and it fits the nature of God's unarmed forces least of all. Moreover, every priest is a public representative of the Church and loyalty to each other needs to have the highest priority in our minds. The Church needs its 'loyal rebels' but not an enemy in the midst.

None of the criteria for selection for ministry refer directly to the ability to manage or organize a church. It doesn't seem a very high-minded calling. Nevertheless, if a church is not well run the gospel ultimately suffers. It's in that light that it's legitimate to plead that all priests have at least a basic expertise in flower arranging – or at least that they know someone who does!

AND FINALLY

Dear God
you have made us for yourself
and our lives forever seek the fullness to be found in you.
Give us grace to work well
        to relish our leisure
        to enjoy our friends
        and to rest content in the knowledge that our
        hearts are stayed on you.
May our lives show the reflection of your beauty,
may our words help others in their search for you,
may our souls at the last find their rest in you,
through Jesus Christ our Lord.
Amen.

17

Life-fulfiller:
Enjoying all God's gifts

———◆———

The priest as a Christian

God's call to a priest comes at a number of levels. If we had to put them in order (which we don't) we would have to say that the first call is to be a human being, the second to be a Christian, and only then, third, to be a priest. My own experience was that the key to the first was the second, and the best way to be the second was the third, but the third step is an exception. I have already quoted Irenaeus, 'The glory of God is a human being fully alive', and this is the central call of our existence, to live life to the full (with a small reserve for emergencies). However, the precious discovery made by millions of people is that being a Christian provides the key to this fascinating prospect. Following Christ is the viewing platform from which the panorama of life makes sense. For a very small proportion of those followers the most appropriate way of fulfilling that calling is by being a priest – the exception. The foundations of this third calling, however, lie in the hauntingly simple invitations to be a human being and to be a Christian. This chapter is a reminder to the priest to stay human! The strange truth is that one of the first signs that we are losing our way is not that we lose our godliness but that we lose our humanity.

Can ministry be enjoyed?

The key question for a priest to answer is this: 'Does my experience of ministry give me life or does it drain life away?' What drew me to faith and then to ministry in the first place was the promise of Jesus that he had come to give people life in all its fullness (John 10.10). I could think of no better way both to experience and to share that life-fullness than by being a priest. I still believe that, but the days of innocence are over. Ministry is extremely demanding, emotionally, spiritually, mentally and physically. Didn't Jesus say that we should love God with all our heart, soul, mind and strength? I've seen the casualties. I've experienced the exhaustion. I've been carried from the field once or twice myself. But I know God still longs that we should live.

One of the most important tasks of a bishop is to ask his priests what he can do to help them enjoy their ministries more, or to make them more fulfilling. Sometimes we might forget as priests that life isn't meant to be an endurance test but a party, a resurrection event anticipating the coming Kingdom. That's not to say that all ministry should be enjoyable. Our ministry at funerals makes that clear very swiftly. Was all Jesus' ministry enjoyable? It was demanding, exhausting and thrilling, all mixed up together. Enjoyment can't be the only measure of ministry. There are bound to be times of failure, boredom, struggle and despair. But if not 'enjoyable', ministry ought to be satisfying, fulfilling, life-enhancing, or at least 'the only way for me to live'. If our head drops too often then something is probably amiss.

The priest has to remember that he or she is in it for the long haul, whether as a parish priest, a self-supporting minister or a minister in secular employment. This isn't a short-term romance but a life-long commitment. Indeed, the analogy with love is instructive because it reminds us that any long-term relationship goes through a number of different stages.

Writing of loving relationships in *Captain Corelli's Mandolin*, Louis de Bernières put it like this:

> Love is a temporary madness, it erupts like volcanoes and then subsides. And when it subsides you have to make a decision. You have to work out whether your roots have so entwined together that it is inconceivable that you should ever part. Because that is what love is. Love is not breathlessness, it is not excitement, it is not the promulgation of promises of eternal passion ... That is just being 'in love', which any fool can do. Love itself is what is left over when being in love has burned away.

It's the same with vocation. Vocation is what's left over when the thrill of being called 'vicar' has long gone. But that vocation is as precious as gold.

Understanding our own needs

The most mysterious person I have to deal with is myself. Getting to understand myself is something to be done with gentleness and patience, but it's sadly possible for priests to spend so much time in other people's lives that they neglect their own. Even time in prayer doesn't guarantee that a priest is in touch with his or her own inner life where the topography may be fragile, volatile or simply unexplored. Time spent on our inner life, sometimes with assistance, is rarely time wasted. Self-awareness is an essential tool of ministry.

One of the danger areas for a priest is the minefield of success and failure. We are always seeking to grow the Kingdom and we work and pray for growth in numbers, in discipleship, in spiritual maturity, and in engagement with society. However, success is very hard to evaluate and church attendance statistics are too crude a measure. For one thing, the outcome may not be in our hands. Major shifts in our culture affect people's church-going habits, for example, and it's hard to buck that deep trend. Moreover, priests work against such an exalted backdrop (the glory of God, the ascended Christ, the coming Kingdom) that failure is inevitable. How can we aspire to such absolutes? Nevertheless, many priests carry a haunting sense of failure on their shoulders because, whatever they try, the normal worldly measures of success seem to indicate a deficit.

It is important to be much more astringent with ourselves about what is really failure in ministry and what, for example, is bruised ego or humiliation. Scripture is more nuanced. The crucifixion was no failure, nor the death of the prophets, although at the time they would have seemed to be so. Paul also was keen to remind the Christians at Corinth that God's foolishness gives quite a different angle on human wisdom (1 Corinthians 1.18–25). Being a faithful witness in a tough situation may put more of a smile on the face of God than a large church that cuts corners with the more challenging demands of the gospel.

Principle number one, then, is not to be afraid of apparent failure. Some of it goes with the territory. It doesn't stop us trying; it just keeps things in perspective. Principle number two is not to be defensive about failure. When something fails it's an opportunity to learn, not an opportunity for self-justification, or re-naming it a 'deferred triumph'. Far better to fail than to skim through ministry without ever touching the sides. The abrasiveness of failure keeps us in touch with our finitude and with God's grace. It also, hopefully, keeps us in touch with our spiritual director and other colleagues and friends. And if it really is our fault, how refreshing it is for others when we say, 'Sorry, my fault!' The people of God are much more ready to forgive than we suspect.

However, the issue of perceived failure is complex. One priest on retirement told his colleagues that he could look back on 'a seamless robe of failure'. I want to protest at such self-denigration. I know that most priests (indeed, most people) carry a vociferous parrot on their shoulder which constantly repeats their failures and weaknesses. 'You could never do that,' says the parrot. 'Others are much better at that than you,' it gleefully assures you. But I believe every priest's ministry is littered with people whose lives have been touched and enriched by what they have said and done – *and they never hear about it.* Television companies multiply their letters of support or complaint by a factor of several hundred to gauge the success of their programmes. Every priest leaves behind them a glittering array of untold stories of lives 'ransomed, healed, restored, forgiven'.

Another dimension of the problem of success and failure is to do with what the Church genteelly calls 'preferment'. For most priests it won't happen. The Church has a structure that is both flat and narrow; there are not very many senior appointments and not a great variety of parallel tracks. Many priests are quite right to believe that they would have made just as good an archdeacon as X; the opportunity simply didn't come. It's necessary, therefore, for priests to forgo the consolations of bitterness and instead to turn positively to other forms of fulfilment. Some of these could be in specialist ministerial interests such as I referred to in Chapter 6, interests that could become 'sixth-day ministries' which enliven the priest and also make a contribution to the wider Church. Why lament not being an archdeacon when you can develop a strong link with an overseas church or have a wide ministry in leading retreats or be a regular visitor to Mount Athos or be much used in the diocese as an *animateur* of debates on climate change and the environment? Hobbies are different from specialist ministerial interests but they too can have a wonderfully enlivening effect. I'm always delighted when I come across priests who have developed remarkable expertise in areas as diverse as rare poultry, Henry VIII, model ship building, quilt-making, off-shore rescue, and fanatical support of lost-cause football teams!

It also needs to be said that priests should never fear a change of direction in ordained ministry. The reasons why we want to be priests at 30 may well be very different from why we want to remain priests at 45 or 55. Our new understandings of ourselves may prompt us to consider quite new ways of expressing our priestly life. Having been a parish priest, must I always be a parish priest? Changes of direction can give a priest new vitality and should be carefully and prayerfully considered with spiritual directors, ministry reviewers and bishops.

Another issue to attend to in our quest for self-understanding as priests is the burden of being good. A priest is a public figure, much observed and often talked about, and the burden of saying the right thing to everyone, handling crises calmly and opposition tactfully, never cursing either the traffic warden or the cat – all this can weigh heavily on his or her shoulders. In the long run it's better to be honest than to wear a mask of impossible reasonableness all the time; honest emotion can be respected and dealt with. It's also important to have some escape routes from 'being good', not in order to behave badly but in order to get off the pedestal and just let the human being play. Priests need places of un-pressured normality. Each of us must find our own.

A trickier set of issues that need attention are 'the devices and desires of our own hearts', with which the priest will need to do some serious business. It can be pretty dark in those corners. Each of us has long fought our own dragons and sought help with our own wounds and we come to ministry with our own record of habitual failings. The emotions these experiences leave us with have to be treated with care and understanding. Repressed emotions can be very dangerous. They can break through into our ministry like a wild, demented relative who we thought was safely in her room, but suddenly bursts into a polite supper party. The question to be asking is, 'What are these deep emotions and desires telling us?' They may be telling us of unresolved wounds and conflicts, or of unarticulated needs for forgiveness and healing, or for intimacy and love. These are the deeper stories to be listening to and the deeper needs to address, with help from spiritual directors and therapists. All dioceses have access to counselling support and wider help is available from, for example, the Society of Mary and Martha in Devon.

No priest needs reminding that we live in an age of much sexual confusion and woundedness, and that priests themselves share some of this bewilderment. Priests are vulnerable because of the nature of their pastoral ministry and because of the stress they are often under. They too need intimacy, but have to realize that boundaries are also part of intimacy, that good relationships need appropriate space or else they suffocate the people involved. The practical implications are spelled out in other publications but what I am concerned with here are the principles, and the chief principle is that we need to understand ourselves and the confusions of our own hearts, and – particularly in this area of sexuality – our extraordinary capacity for self-deception.

Loving the people who love us

If the priest is married the family is his or her first church. The priest's main responsibility is to the family's well-being. In the ordination service the bishop asks the candidate, 'Will you endeavour to fashion your own life and that of your household according to the way of Christ?' The question could sound somewhat negative and controlling unless it's taken in its richest meaning: 'Will you endeavour to live together in such a way that you enjoy the glorious liberty of the children of God?'

Michael dismissed St Valentine's Day as mere commercialism

God wants all his children to flourish and I'm sure he has a deep concern for the families and loved ones of his priests, who do sometimes get it wrong.

The first task of a married priest, therefore, is to guard the freedom of his or her spouse. The gift of our life partner is God's greatest mercy and that gift needs to be protected from the slings and arrows of ministry's outrageous fortune. Partners need to have the freedom to pursue their own careers, to be involved in parish work only as they wish, to love their spouse and their children before anything else, to have a Sunday off, to sunbathe in the back garden, to swear when necessary – *to be their own child of God*. In all fairness, the priest cannot be pastor to his or her spouse, but the priest's responsibility is to make sure the marriage flourishes, so the planning of treats, meals out, breaks and holidays need to be high in the family priorities. The three key gifts a clergy couple need to give each other are time, communication and kindness. I write these again – time, communication and kindness. I was shaky on all three when I started out in ministry with a new wife and a world to save. The world was less impressed with me than I wished, and my wife probably was as well. She was very forgiving and we took time to communicate kindly with each other. We've been negotiating ever since.

What applies to a priest and his or her spouse also applies to the children. You desperately want them to have the afore-mentioned 'glorious liberty of the children of God', but you are not God and they are not the Holy Family! They too need their freedom to be guarded. They didn't choose to live in a goldfish bowl or to have their home invaded regularly, or their parents in and out at all times and their mealtimes constantly inter-rupted by the telephone. Some children love the involvement, the sense of being at the heart of things; for others it's a deep embarrassment. Again, time, communication and kindness are the essential gifts. I shall forever regret that I didn't give my children more time in those fascinating formative years. They have been wonderfully forgiving.

The issue of time has cropped up in both the preceding paragraphs. The problem with the task of ministry is that it is infinite, and the only person who can make it finite is the priest himself or herself. It follows that the negotiation of time is crucial. No-one can manufacture any more time than anyone else. A week has 168 hours and no more. People have begun to talk in terms of a notional 50-hour working week for priests – 40 hours as in other jobs and 10 that a committed lay person might well devote to church-related activities. I dislike getting into such tallies but I recognize the value for others. In any case, in order to build in recovery time from a very demanding job, holidays, days off and any other breaks should go into the diary first, as absolute priorities. This is followed by time for a retreat and any other quiet days or reading and reflection days, which are part of the priest's regime for staying fit and well. Days off should, if at all possible, follow the example of the Jewish sabbath and start the previous evening, and if there has been a particularly heavy schedule of work for a while, some compensation time should be taken (this is the reason for the usual short breaks after Christmas and Easter). I'm in danger of becoming very prescriptive here – I simply write out of concern and poor personal performance!

The situation of a single priest is just as difficult to negotiate. The same issues of time apply but (as for many women priests) with the added complication of all the extra time needed for domestic tasks. For many single priests, closing the door at night brings both relief and loneliness and it's essential to guard time for those special friends who bring balance and respite to pressurized lives. Stories are told of congregations being less aware of the needs of single priests, and sometimes less forgiving. Whereas the need of a married priest to see his family is understood, the need of a single priest to keep in touch with life outside the parish is less acknowledged. It may be good for a single priest to take two or three days off together, for example, to be able to make the journey to see family and special friends. The principle is, as ever: we need to be kind to ourselves. Love your neighbour *as yourself.*

The issue of friendships within the parish lurks behind some of what I've written in this section. Conventional priestly wisdom has it that you can't have particular friends in the parish for fear of jealousy, 'vicar's cliques', and problems with confidentiality. I tend to be heretical on this, probably because I've been lucky, but it seems to me that to cut ourselves off from friendships in this way is to detract from the very humanness we are trying to model in Christian community. Friendships arise naturally as we make our way through life and need be received gladly as gifts from God's hand, wherever they come from. Priests simply need to be wise about when and where they meet their friends and what they talk about, as would any other 'caring professional'.

Cutting to the chase

If there were a set of answers on how to flourish as a human being while also living with the distinctive pressures of being a priest, we would all have found them long ago. There is no secret out there awaiting our discovery. Every January since I was ordained I have approached the new year with the sublime confidence that 'this time I've got it sussed'. Each year I learn a fraction more about my lack of realism. Nevertheless, my experience of ministry is that it's immensely satisfying and usually very enjoyable, and it's a great privilege to be able to live on the basis of our fundamental convictions and to share with others the excitement, traumas, and questions of the Christian journey. Occasionally I meet someone who looks and feels defeated by the complexity of the ministerial task today. Priests can be ground down by the 'multiple overwhelmings' (David Ford) and the relentless reactivity of parish life. They can also be dispirited by the sheer banality of some aspects of ministry compared with the high idealism with which they entered ministry years before. Let's face it – ministry can be boring.

The place to go to when that happens is the sacred hearth of faith where the blazing reality of God forever burns, and to the stubborn fact of God's call to us to serve him *here*, in this very place, now. When ministry is hard and people seem unresponsive to our most stirring oratory and most brilliant ideas, that isn't the time to mutter darkly about 'an evil and adulterous generation' and ask the bishop for a move. Rather, it's a time to return to the confidence that God has called us to be here, now, and nowhere else. God believes in us more than we believe in ourselves. In calling us to be in a particular place, he works even through the bewildering and arcane processes of the Church. God is in the facts. We need to trust them. Moreover, we have this high, thrilling and dangerous calling to be 'thin' people, on the boundary of heaven and earth, handling the high beauty of Bible, sacrament and prayer. Why should we want to do anything else?

In the ordination service the bishop says to the candidates: 'We trust that long ago you began to weigh and ponder all this . . .' Well, yes, we did, and, many years on, by far the majority of clergy would still say that the best decision they could ever have made was to accept God's call to the life and work of a priest.

Further resources

This is a personal, somewhat idiosyncratic, collection of recommended further reading and resources. It simply lists some of the books that have helped me in my own thinking about priestly ministry.

Books on priesthood

Wesley Carr, *The Priestlike Task* (SPCK, 1985).

Andrew Clitherow, *Renewing Faith in Ordained Ministry* (SPCK, 2004).

Christopher Cocksworth and Rosalind Brown, *Being a Priest Today* (Canterbury Press, 2002).

Steven Croft, *Ministry in Three Dimensions* (DLT, 1999).

Robin Greenwood, *Transforming Priesthood* (SPCK, 1994).

George Guiver et al., *The Fire and the Clay* (SPCK, 1993).

David Ison (ed.), *The Vicar's Guide* (Church House Publishing, 2005).

Michael Ramsey, *The Christian Priest Today* (SPCK, first pub. 1972).

Alastair Redfern, *Ministry and Priesthood* (DLT, 1999).

2 Presiding genius?

Paul Bradshaw (ed.), *Companion to Common Worship* (SPCK, 2001).

Stephen Conway (ed.), *Living the Eucharist* (DLT, 2001).

Peter Craig-Wild, *Tools for Transformation* (DLT, 2002).

Mark Earey and Gilly Myers (eds), *Common Worship Today* (HarperCollins, 2001).

Richard Giles, *Creating Uncommon Worship* (Canterbury Press, 2004).

Michael Perham, *Liturgy Pastoral and Parochial* (SPCK, first pub. 1984).

Mike Riddell et al., *The Prodigal Project* (SPCK, 2000).

Pete Ward (ed.), *Mass Culture* (BRF, 1999).

3 Spiritual explorer

All the spiritual classics, old and new!

Andrew Clitherow, *Into Your Hands* (SPCK, 2001).
Judy Hirst, *Struggling To Be Holy* (DLT, 2006).
Eugene Peterson, *Under the Unpredictable Plant* (Eerdmans, 1992).

4 Artful story-teller

David Buttrick, *Homiletic* (SCM, 1987).
Fred Craddock, *Preaching* (Abingdon Press, 1985).
David Day, *A Preaching Workbook* (SPCK, 1998).
David Day, *Embodying the Word* (SPCK, 2005).
Geoffrey Stevenson (ed.), *Pulpit Journeys* (DLT, 2006).

5 Multilingual interpreter

Joan Bakewell (ed.), *Belief* (BBC, 2005).
Sylvia Collins-Mayo et al., *Making Sense of Generation Y* (Church House Publishing, 2006).
John Drane, *Cultural Change and Biblical Faith* (Paternoster, 2000).
John Drane, *Do Christians Know How To Be Spiritual?* (DLT, 2005).
Michael Paul Gallagher, *Dive Deeper* (DLT, 2001).
Richard Harries, *God Outside the Box* (SPCK, 2002).
Alister McGrath, *Bridge-building* (IVP, 1992).
Bel Mooney (ed.), *Devout Sceptics* (Hodder and Stoughton, 2003).
John Pritchard, *How to Explain your Faith* (SPCK, 2006).

6 Inquisitive learner

Any theological books that take your eye!

Paul Ballard and John Pritchard, *Practical Theology in Action* (SPCK, 2nd edn, 2006).

7 Pain bearer

Margaret Spufford, *Celebration* (Fount, 1989).
W. H. Vanstone, *Love's Endeavour, Love's Expense* (DLT, 1977).
Miroslav Volf, *Free of Charge* (Zondervan, 2005).
Nicholas Wolterstorff, *Lament for a Son* (SPCK, 1997).

8 Wounded companion

Christopher Moody, *Eccentric Ministry* (DLT, 1992).
Eugene Peterson, *Working the Angles* (Eerdmans, 1993).
Peter Shaw, *Conversation Matters* (Continuum, 2005).
Peter Speck, *Being There* (SPCK, 1988).

9 Weather-beaten witness

Commission on Urban Life and Faith, *Faithful Cities* (Church House Publishing and Methodist Publishing House, 2006).
Ann Morisy, *Journeying Out* (Morehouse, 2004).
Jim Wallis, *Faith Works* (SPCK, 2002).

11 Friendly irritant

Marina Cantacuzino, *The F Word* (The Forgiveness Project, 2005).
Piers McGrandle, *Trevor Huddleston: Turbulent Priest* (Continuum, 2004).
Miroslav Volf, *Exclusion and Embrace* (Abingdon Press, 1996).
Walter Wink, *Engaging the Powers* (Fortress Press, 1992).

12 Creative leader

John Adair and John Nelson, *Creative Church Leadership* (Canterbury Press, 2004).
Stephen R. Covey, *The Seven Habits of Highly Effective People* (Simon and Schuster, 1992).
Richard Higginson, *Transforming Leadership* (SPCK, 2002).
James Jones and Andrew Goddard, *The Moral Leader* (IVP, 2002).
Walter C. Wright, *Relational Leadership* (Paternoster, 2000).

13 Attractive witness

Steven Croft et al., *Evangelism in a Spiritual Age* (Church House Publishing, 2005).
Bob Mayo et al., *Ambiguous Evangelism* (SPCK, 2004).
Brian McLaren, *More Ready Than You Realise* (Zondervan, 2002).
Philip Richter and Leslie Francis, *Gone But Not Forgotten* (DLT, 1998).
Mike Riddell, *Deep Stuff* (Lion, 1999).
David Smith, *Mission after Christendom* (DLT, 2003).
Graham Tomlin, *The Provocative Church* (SPCK, 2002).

14 Faith coach

Rob Bell, *Velvet Elvis* (Zondervan, 2005).

Mark Greene, *Supporting Christians at Work* (London Institute for Contemporary Christianity, 2001).

Gerard Hughes, *God of Surprises* (DLT, 1985).

15 Mature risk-taker

Steven Croft, *Transforming Communities* (DLT, 2002).

Steven Croft (ed.), *The Future of the Parish System* (Church House Publishing, 2006).

John Drane, *The McDonaldisation of the Church* (DLT, 2000).

Bob Jackson, *The Road to Growth* (Church House Publishing, 2005).

Mission-shaped Church Working Group, *Mission-shaped Church* (Church House Publishing, 2004).

Mission-shaped Church Working Group, *Mission-shaped Parish, Children, Spirituality, and Rural* (Church House Publishing, 2006).

Michael Moynagh, *emergingchurch.intro* (Monarch, 2004).

Stuart Murray, *Post-Christendom* (Paternoster, 2004).

Nick Page, *The Church Invisible* (Zondervan, 2004).

Nick Spencer, *Parochial Vision* (Paternoster, 2004).

Pete Ward, *Liquid Church* (Paternoster, 2002).

16 Flower arranger

Roger and Stephen Allen, *Winnie-the-Pooh on Management and Problem Solving* (Methuen, 1998).

John Nelson, *Management and Ministry* (Modem, 1996).

John Nelson (ed.), *Leading, Managing, Ministering* (Modem, 1999).

17 Life-fulfiller

Henri Nouwen, *The Return of the Prodigal Son* (DLT, 1994).

Yvonne Warren, *The Cracked Pot* (Kevin Mayhew, 2002).